NATHAN GRIL

S. JOSHUA S\

FAITHFUL

— IS —

SUCCESSFUL

NOTES
TO THE
DRIVEN
PILGRIM

outskirtspress
DENVER, COLORADO

To Dennis and Eileen Bakke

Table of Contents

God in the Work: How can faith and work be integrated to make a difference?

Preface

This book project was initiated in response to requests from a select group of outstanding Christians in graduate or professional school. Under the Harvey Fellowship program, these students had been given the privilege of engaging with older successful Christian professionals during a week-long summer institute in Washington, D.C. These Christian professionals were accomplished in fields in which being a Christian was rare. Among them were filmmakers, artists, academics, and bench scientists. Each presenter had been asked to discuss what difference it made that they were a Christian in their field. The speakers described how they thought about integrating faith into their vocation and their experiences doing so. The talks were very human. Speakers detailed creative and beautiful ways faith manifested itself in work. But speakers were realistic in describing uncertainties and failures.

These students found it incredibly helpful to have the speakers kick off conversations about integrating faith and vocation and have examples of what this looks like in the lives of committed Christians working in their own fields. For many, it was the first time that they had thought very seriously about what difference being a Christian meant in their vocation. For others, it provided a model, perhaps a competing model, of what integrating faith and vocation looked like.

At the end of the week-long program, Justin Denholm (who played a significant role in the book's development) and several other students asked us to consider putting together a volume, collecting material such as what was presented because it would be useful for others who did not have a similar structured opportunity to reflect on these issues. We agreed to compile an edited book of writings by Christians who had achieved acclaim in their area. We started by soliciting chapters from people that had participated in these institutes over the previous twenty years. Thirteen authors responded to the invitation. They graciously gave and took feedback from one another. We asked authors to keep the chapters brief but gave authors some flexibility to write on the various elements of being a Christian in the professional and academic workplace. The authors that volunteered are from different fields—an artist, a literary critic, an expert in Islamic law, a biologist—and at different stages in their careers.

All the authors are what would be considered professionally successful, although we hesitate to use this term since God's definition of success is quite different from common definitions of success. Our job as editors was to take the chapters and make them cohere together. Fortunately, this was an easy task since one overarching theme emerged; and this is reflected in the book title: *Faithful is Successful*. This theme showed up over and over again in the chapters as the authors described how they had come to the realization that God's definition of success differed from their own and that of their peers. Chapters describe how our desire for professional success can insidiously supplant our desire to be faithful. We rationalize our ambition, sometimes subconsciously, by telling ourselves that we have a specific vocational calling and that he will use our success for His glory. And He may, but often it is our own glory we are seeking.

Does this mean that we should not strive for excellence, to reach the pinnacle of our chosen professions? Clearly not. Indeed, many of the authors have attained esteemed positions and achieved significantly. But, this is why this book is valuable. The chapters are intended to provoke reflection and conversation about faith and vocation, about calling, and about the pursuit of excellence. The book includes the insightful reflections of mature Christians on the mystery of calling, reconciling faith and personal ambition, and how God makes a difference in work. Throughout their careers each author has had to personally reconcile such tensions and this lived experience grounds the discussion in this book.

The summer institutes, like the one where the book idea originated, are organized by the Harvey Fellows Program. The Harvey Fellows Program is sponsored by the Mustard Seed Foundation and funded by the generous support of Dennis and Eileen Bakke. It is a fellowship program for promising Christian graduate students entering fields where Christians are historically underrepresented. The Bakkes started the program in the early 1990s to help Christians entering positions of influence in society and culture and prepare them for the work they would do there. The Bakkes themselves have thought hard about what integrating faith and vocation looks like in business and education and wanted others to do the same in their chosen vocations. The Bakkes' own thinking is best reflected in Dennis's well-documented tenure at Applied Energy Services and his book, *Joy at Work* (PVG, 2005).

Over the years, hundreds of students in fields from furniture design to finance have been assisted in their graduate studies and their efforts to think carefully and creatively about the integration of faith and vocation. Fellows can be found in government, academia, business, and the arts, working to redeem broken institutions and structures to make them work better for the people they serve and to reflect God's goodness in Christ. We ourselves were fortunate enough to have received one of these fellowships. We benefited from the financial support and the patient help with thinking about integrating faith and vocation. We have also benefited very much from knowing Dennis and Eileen and witnessing their family's great example of lives graciously lived. Receiving these fellowships affirmed our calling and marked us in important ways. We are grateful to the Bakkes and dedicate this book to them.

Introduction: Faithful is Successful

Nathan Grills
University of Melbourne
Australia

David E. Lewis
Vanderbilt University
United States

S. Joshua Swamidass
Washington University, St. Louis
United States

1. Introduction

"Therefore, I urge you, brothers, in view of God's mercy, to offer your bodies as living sacrifices, holy and pleasing to God—this is your spiritual act of worship" (Romans 12:1).

God wants all of our lives. In response to what God has done for us, we are encouraged to offer our whole selves for God's use and purposes. Motivated by God's unfailing love, best reflected in Jesus' sacrifice, do we turn around and give ourselves to God, not in part but in whole? We are to live for Christ from our waking to our sleeping and during our week and on our weekends. God's presence is to be with us during our work and our play.

Most Christians readily agree with this idea that God has asked for our lives in their entirety. A smaller number have thought carefully about what this means in the context of their specific vocation, whether it is law, sales, construction, or some other work. Some who have thought about it ponder it in the context of doing what they do with integrity and a good work ethic. We would be doing well in our vocations even if this is all that marked our work as distinctive. Yet few of us can say that our work is defined by these traits.

But integrating faith and vocation is much more than this. The Christian gospel is about God transforming our lives through the work of His Spirit in salvation. It is unsurprising that He wants to influence not only how we do what we do, but also what we do. This includes influencing our choice of vocation and what our lives in those vocations look like. Where we fail to adequately integrate faith and vocation we miss opportunities to reflect God's glory in this world.

When God calls Christians to specific vocations, he wants them to think about how they can do what they do "Christianly," and to creatively explore what difference being a Christian makes in their vocation. God's redemptive work in the world includes the social and cultural institutions that provide the context of their lives, including vocations and professions. Unless Christians think consciously about the integration of their faith into their work, they will adopt the patterns and norms of work in the world around them. They will also miss out on the opportunity to creatively transform their world of work into something more beautiful and more honoring to God.

Some Christians will resist the idea that their faith has much to say about the substance of what they do, particularly those where vocations have clear boundaries and strong norms. It is not immediately clear how to do literary criticism, bench science, or hedge fund investing in a distinctly Christian way that is both sacred and excellent. A resistance to being labeled a "Christian _____ [fill in the vocation]" is understandable because simplistic answers in integrating faith and vocation often come across as trite and unrealistic. However, this does not mean that a person engaged in these professions and enervated by the Holy Spirit cannot figure out how this is possible. Indeed, many of the chapters of this volume include beautiful examples of integrating faith and vocation in unexpected and exciting ways.

Perhaps, the most impactful aspect to integrating of faith and vocation comes simply from living a life authentically changed by the Holy Spirit and is played out as we live and follow Christ. This might mean that we prioritize our own spiritual walk, the needs of our family and our roles at church above our achievements at work. Other parts of this integration come as the result of conscious choices (also Spirit-led) made to try to integrate faith and vocation.

In Christian circles there has been a renewed interest in examining how faith and work are to be integrated. Some of this work takes a second look at the writings of the Protestant reformers for insights. Others focus on specific ways that faith may influence work, such as seeing work as a means of furthering God's purposes for social justice in the world or seeing the workplace as a place for sharing one's faith. Fewer recent works describe efforts by Christians to integrate faith and work in specific professional vocations.

The purpose of this book is to help Christians think about what it means to integrate faith and vocation. People find themselves in different kinds of work--blue collar or white collar, in the home or in the church or marketplace. Some people have a choice over what they do. Some have had a sense of God's calling into one vocation or another. Others find themselves in work that is difficult but necessary to make a living. This book introduces readers to people working in different professional fields who have thought consciously about what difference their faith makes to their work. They are persons generally engaged in mental rather than manual work and they have had some choice in occupation. This is by no means the norm in our world or in world history. The insights of the book's chapters can apply broadly to persons working in various contexts but are probably most applicable to Christians entering similar professional fields as the chapter authors.

Our hope is that this book will fill a gap by providing readers real-life examples from Christians in different vocations, describing how they have sought to integrate faith and work. The thirteen chapters provide a vehicle for thoughtful Christians with academic and professional credentials to share their wisdom and experience in this endeavor. The chapters vary in approach. Some are more theological and others are more testimonial. Some are rooted in specific disciplines and others deal with more general issues. Authors address a number of key questions. How have they thought about integrating faith and vocation? What problems have they encountered? What would they say to a younger version of themselves now in hindsight? The chapters are surprising in their creativity and insight. The authors are also disarmingly frank and humble. For most of the contributors the chapters provide partial and tentative answers to the questions posed. They are intended to be the beginning of a conversation rather than the final word.

While the book is a conversation, it has the virtue of being a structured conversation where the authors get the first word. A thematic consistency arose organically as the editors explored the thoughtful and wise responses of the authors. One insightful overarching theme emerged from the authors' reflections about being a successful Christian in their field: Being faithful is being successful. This definition of success is distinctly different from what others in our respective disciplines would define as 'successful'. The three sub-themes that emerged were around the mysteries of calling (The Mystery of Calling), faith and ambition (Success and Ambition), and how God influences the substance of our work (God in the Work). The book is organized into three sections corresponding to these sub-themes.

2. Faithful is Successful

The overarching theme of the book is the book's title: faithful is successful. The title has a double meaning. First, what ultimate success means is to faithfully follow Christ. Many of the authors refer to a trap whereby the drive for professional success can supplant this ultimate goal. Unfortunately, our Church leaders, Christian friends and even our Christian families often value our professional success over being faithful in our work. Perhaps we think that success in our discipline will bring glory to God, and bring people to God as they see what amazing people we are. We tell ourselves that God wants us to be successful, to achieve in our professions, to get the next publication or to have a profitable year. Perhaps, but there is an incredible danger of losing sight of what our aim is—to walk with Christ and serve him faithfully—in our headlong pursuit of what others would consider success.

In fact, Christians can fail. It was surprising to us that many of the 'successful' Christians who were asked to contribute to this book chose to write about their terrific failures and focused on what it means to fail successfully. The Scriptures include a number of stories about the faithful whose lives are not successful by any worldly standard. For example, Jeremiah and Hosea are ridiculed and marginalized because of their faithfulness. Those that would be considered worldly successes, like Daniel or Joseph, were press-ganged into service and kidnapped and jailed, respectively, prior to their rise in power and position. Similarly, the chapters inside this volume meditate on whether God has called us to success in our professions relative to other callings in our lives. They also explore how professional success comes with real pitfalls for our faith. Each of the authors has experienced professional success and the chapters poignantly describe the difficulties figuring out the proper place of ambition in their faith. As Nathan Grills' chapter asks, whose glory are we seeking? What matters in the end is faithfulness rather than success. If readers come away with one theme from the book, this is the one we would choose.

The second meaning of the title is that our fullness as persons and workers is only realized in faithfulness. Who we are intended to be and what we can be at our best can only be realized when Christ is at work in us. This is because God's design for us is both defined and executed by God himself. What does it mean to be a Christian researcher, programmer, or physician? To some extent, we can only know by living faithfully and letting God have his way in us. We cannot experience fully what God has for us in our professions apart from him. Not all Christian professors, furniture designers, or musicians look the same and what unique form of this you or I will take can only manifest itself under the gracious hand of God's supervision. When we are faithful, this eases the road of God's creative work in us, makes smooth the road for God to make us into who he wants us to be. If there is such a thing as calling to a vocation at all, its manifestation is intimately tied to faithfulness.

So how do we explain when those without faith achieve excellent things- some of which seem to be God-glorifying. For example, take the discovery of antibiotics. This excellent work of those without faith has transformed and saved the lives of billions of people. Would God's presence in the filmmaker or scientist who has chosen not to follow God have made their work better? This is a question we cannot answer fully here. Let us note, however, that many persons whose aims have been different and whose hearts have been shaped by other forces have exemplified excellence. We cannot observe the counterfactual—what those persons would be like with lives submitted consciously to God. What we can do is thank God for the excellence we see, a gift of grace and a reflection of his image. God has apportioned to different people gifts and talents and abilities. God has given to each of us a measure of excellence, perhaps some more than others, or in a form that is more visible than others. Our claim is that this excellence undiluted is more likely to be on display when God is at work in us. This does not mean, however, that this excellence is not on display without God or that God cannot demonstrate his excellence in the faithless.

3. The Mystery of Calling

For many Christians the challenge of integrating faith and vocation is one of letting faith influence the big picture questions of vocation. The arc of our personal history should be bent in Christ's direction. This means that the overarching plan of our lives is to be shaped by the transforming power of Christ in us. Many Christians are more comfortable in thinking about how to live for Christ day-to-day than allowing their faith to shape the larger questions of vocation. They pray and meditate about how to reflect Christ in their upcoming visit to relatives or during their current trial. Of course, being faithful in the day-to-day activities is central to the Christian walk but faith should also shape our vocational ambitions and our lives as workers.

In this section of the book we address the mysteries of calling, of finding a vocation and involving God in the overall plan for one's life. The authors present diverse views on how calling has worked itself out in their lives. They address the following questions: What is calling? Called to what? How can we know it? Does it change? How important is it? A surprising number of the authors took circuitous routes to their current field or job. What they thought was a clear calling turned out to not be so clear after all. Some thought they were called to one type of job or position, only to have that change. For others, divining what it was that God called them to do was a difficult and lengthy process. And, those that had a clear calling often encountered circumstances that made success in that vocation difficult, but success in other spheres more possible.

Bryan T. McGraw writes both about the importance of vocation for the Christian but also how rare it is for Christians to know exactly what God has for them in advance. McGraw traces his own winding career path and how he ended up doing something he had not anticipated doing. He notes that sometimes the best we can do is "muddle through," attempting to live faithfully where we are rather than struggling to reconfigure things to involve ourselves in a situation where we can do what we think God really wants us to be doing. McGraw notes that we should neither despise the circumstances that keep us from doing what we feel called to do nor be prisoners to those circumstances.

Dano Jukanovich describes a similarly winding path to his current position. He had clear plans for what he hoped to accomplish as a type-A business school graduate. Fifteen years later God has redirected his path, sometimes through wrenching failure, to his current position in a private equity firm in Rwanda. Jukanovich notes that his life now is much better than he could have imagined it fifteen years ago. He describes beautifully how he has learned that God has called us to "full-time life." God calls us to a relationship with him that integrates who we are, where we live, what we do, and with whom we do it.

David E. Lewis takes up a theme that other chapters also address, namely that there are many models of integrating faith and vocation in specific disciplines. Lewis describes the picture he had in his own head as an undergraduate as to what a Christian professor would look like. He then proceeds to detail the ways that, neither he nor other faithful Christian faculty he knows, fit that mold. Rather, Lewis argues, God's creative work of faith in each has generated different and creative models for what a faithful Christian looks like in the academy.

Howard Louthan provides a beautiful account of a clear vocational calling but outlines the challenges associated with pursuing that calling in the messiness of life. Louthan, a historian, describes his life with his wife (also an academic) and their twins. His chapter describes the ways in which pursuing professional success and the demands of being faithful to family and church can come into conflict. Louthan, borrowing from a metaphor from Vaclav Havel, describes the Christian as a dissident. Our choices to be faithful in cases where faithfulness and vocational success come into conflict challenge the very foundation of the vocations and world in which we participate. When we conform or remain silent we give silent approval to the larger system built on false premises and values.

The four chapters provide a helpful base for the remaining two sections to build on. Each author deals with how to let God be involved in the larger vocational choices that so characterize many of our lives. Each also hints at the difficulties addressed more fully in the next section around reconciling faith and a drive for professional success.

4. Success and Ambition

Central to a book dealing with the integration of faith and vocation is addressing how faith relates to ambition. Indeed, many of the chapters throughout the book describe the fraught relationship between our faith in Jesus and ambition. In this section the reader is pressed to think consciously about their own definition of success and how it squares with scriptural understandings. Authors also grapple with the place of ambition for vocational success and how it squares with God's calling on our lives. The pursuit of professional success can so insidiously supplant other callings on our lives. The uncomfortable truth is that sometimes God does not call us to be successful in our professions but to be faithful to our multiple callings including church, family, and friends.

Justin Denholm provides a provocative theological reflection on success and ambition. On the definition of success, he notes that there are many examples from Scriptures of persons serving God faithfully that are not professionally successful. He also calls into question whether our work is a vocation that should be privileged over other forms of service and raises the issue of multiple vocations or callings. Denholm also writes about the misapplication of the parable of the talents to individual skills and abilities. He notes that in context the parable is for the church rather than individuals. If we are to steward our gifts and abilities as individuals at all, he argues, it should be to help the church be a good steward of the Earth and its people.

Matthew Cabeen's chapter addresses the conflicts that can arise between the drive for professional success and other callings on the Christian's life, notably family life. Cabeen's chapter pushes us to think consciously about what we mean when we talk about a "successful career." He describes how what is good for one's career often means "what I want for me" rather than the other people implicated in decisions about career, such as spouses and children. Cabeen details how goals for a vibrant family life and a successful career can come into conflict and he provides helpful advice to make such big decisions when those goals come into conflict.

Bruce Huber addresses the tension for the Christian between faith and ambition. On the one hand, ambition fuels accomplishment. The success in worldly affairs that results from ambition can accomplish great good. On the other hand, Christians find ambition counter to Christian character in that it can consist of self-promotion and selfishness termed acceptably as life strategy. Huber describes how ambition, rightly understood, can emerge as a consequence of rather than a competitor to obedience to Christ. Ultimately, Christ and his church should be the object of our ambition.

Nathan Grills explores how we can approach both success and failure faithfully. He discusses how our identity becomes wrapped up in success and likens it to an illicit drug. It can temporarily make us happy by filling the void in our hearts left by an incomplete awareness of our value and meaning in Christ. Markers of professional success such as a publication in a leading journal are a quick hit to which we can become emotionally and psychologically addicted. He describes how the drive for success unchecked can supplant our identity in Christ. Using examples from his own life and work, he explains how disability and failure can actually be a severe mercy for successful Christians.

Perhaps more than any section of this book, this section highlights the primary theme of the book by asking readers to determine what ultimate success looks like and how it squares with the ultimate ambition of walking with Christ and serving him. For some chapter authors the answer to the question of how to square professional success and faith has a distinctive answer based upon their specific vocation and this is explored further in the final section.

5. God in the Work

In the final section of the book we examine how faith and vocation can be integrated, using the insights of practitioners in diverse fields. Here we hear from different authors who write about how their faith influences both what they do and how they do what they do. Each author addresses what it means to participate in their field in a distinctly Christian way. Does it make a difference that a hedge fund manager, literary critic, international development practitioner, Islamic scholar, or artist is a Christian? Our conclusion is yes, but not always in the manner, or to the degree, that we and others might have anticipated.

Here the authors address misconceptions and share insights from efforts to actively integrate faith into what we do. The chapters reveal that some aspects of doing what we do Christianly follow similar courses across different vocations. Integrity will mean something slightly different in distinct vocations. Loving our co-workers will look different, depending upon who our co-workers are and what they need. Yet, the admonition drawn from Scripture that compels us is the same. In some vocations, however, the demands of the vocation lend themselves to opportunities for integrating faith and vocation in ways that are specific to the vocation. These chapters explain how.

Soo Chuen Tan discusses the way he has thought about his faith and his job as a finance professional. He describes his struggle in the midst of Wall Street scandals to determine whether it was actually possible to live a Christ-centered life as a hedge fund manager. Was he really called to this? Ultimately, Tan decided that this is what he was called to do and started his own investment firm. He describes how he attempted to reconcile his faith with the structure and practice of the new firm. Tan discusses some of the real challenges he has faced in the firm from deciding a fair fee structure to deciding if certain types of investments are off limits. Ultimately, he concludes that living out his faith in this world requires tremendous discernment and that this can only come from daily walking by faith.

Caleb Spencer's chapter addresses the question of whether there is such a thing as Christian literary criticism. Working through four different models of the way that faith might work its way into literary critical work, Spencer argues that Christianity makes little, if any, principled difference to literary critical work. He does not deny the possibility that the Holy Spirit reveals insights to individuals but suggests this is better understood as a peculiar moment of grace, perhaps also accessible to non-Christians, rather than the basis for theorizing about collective Christian responsibility in criticism.

Spencer concludes that what is true for the literary critic that is a Christian is that, like other Christians, they are the hands and feet of Christ in the world around them.

Laura S. Meitzner Yoder highlights four lessons learned about integrating faith and vocation as a person engaged in teaching and community-based research on environmental issues in Southeast Asia. She describes what she has learned about the special opportunities expatriate academics have in remote conflict zones. Persons in these positions have the opportunity to hear local and minority voices and witness models of the integration of faith and public life foreign to persons living in the secularized West. Yoder also describes the difficulties and opportunities associated with developing trust in conflict zones. Finally, she describes how God's work often happens in the interruptions to what we are trying to accomplish. Yoder concludes that we are called to suspend our desire for carefully calculated career trajectories, even to get something big done for God, in order to participate in God's larger plan for redemption.

David R. Vishanoff describes how one metaphor, sacrificial listening, has influenced his choice of topics, his mode of research, and his practical pedagogy as a religious studies professor. He details his own personal journey to graduate school in religious studies and how he developed a passion for understanding the Other. Vishanoff describes how his pedagogy and research are shaped by the agendas of three sets of Others, his students, the secular academy, and Muslim intellectuals. In these tasks Vishanoff explains how genuine listening, a relentless attempt to understand others, shapes his life and vocation.

Sarah Awad discusses the integration of faith and vocation in the way that it influences specific challenges associated with artists living between the church and the art world. She identifies three challenges—loneliness, ambition, and bitterness. Awad details how a lack of understanding about art in the church can be alienating for the artist. One of the places where the artist needs to feel most at home is also a place where she is least understood. Awad describes how art is a performance-driven field and how this field requires the artist to achieve, often by getting affirmation and recognition of one's work. The artist needs a certain amount of ego to participate in the risks associated with the profession. Yet, how does one square this aspect of the work with the humility required in Scripture? Artists also confront bitterness when expectations are unmet and when peers, better and worse than you, are promoted above you. Awad describes how she has dealt with these three challenges and concludes that desiring God first is a crucial step to gaining artistic freedom.

Together, these three sections provide an opportunity for Christians working in fields where there are few Christians to pass along what they have learned. Through these twelve chapters we demonstrate that integrating faith and vocation is possible, exciting, and often happens in diverse and yet to be discovered ways. The chapters offer many points of commonality, although depicted through quite distinctive approaches to integration of faith and vocation. In common, we suggest the primacy of faithfulness first and then address the various ways that faith influences both the how and the what of vocation. Collectively we illustrate the mystery of vocational calling, the important and difficult relationship between faith and ambition, and God's intimate involvement in our work.

However, the chapters will reveal that authors do not all agree on the details of how faith and vocation can and should be integrated. This is where we invite you into our conversation and suggest that you engage with us in thinking about how best to integrate your faith and vocation.

Seeing What's Around: Vision and Vocation

Bryan T. McGraw
Wheaton College
Wheaton, IL
USA

I went to college to prepare for a career as a spy. It's true. My classes often chuckle when I mention this, no doubt believing I am embroidering the truth a bit. But when I chose classes in the summer of 1989, ready to start at Vanderbilt that fall, I signed up for Russian because I thought it would be the most helpful language for my career as the real embodiment of characters in popular espionage novels. The fall of the Berlin wall that autumn (among many other factors) derailed that plan, but I had others, plenty of them. In none of them did I envision myself teaching political theory at Wheaton College, a relatively small Christian liberal arts college located in Chicago's western suburbs.

In what follows, I want to use my experience of landing in unexpected places and doing unexpected things as an occasion to reflect on the idea of vocation and calling. All Christians understand that our deepest calling is to live faithfully as recipients of God's grace and mercy, and we should understand that such a calling includes our everyday lives. Living faithfully is not just a matter of proper worship or affirming the right doctrines (though those are important). It is also a matter of living out our "secular" lives, the parts of our lives we share with all. How to be a banker, a lawyer, a nurse or a carpenter is part of the life of faith, not something to the side of it. So to think about vocation is to consider what we should be doing with ourselves in spheres of life that we share with all, concerns that often do not differ from what our neighbors and friends outside the faith share with us when thinking about their careers and life choices. But what makes vocation different for the Christian, distinguishing it from mere career, is that it is freighted with our sense of participation in God's work, His kingdom-work. To think about vocation is to consider how our secular lives ought to reflect and participate in God's providential care in the world at large: what are we called to do in the world as part of what God is already doing?

For many (perhaps most), this means trying to get a long-range vision for your life and a detailed, executable plan for how to get there. I once had a student who, in her first advising session here at Wheaton, sat down in a chair opposite me, flipped open a laptop and proceeded to describe how her color-coded Excel spreadsheet showed how she could complete a double-major in three years and set herself up for a career in the State Department. She knew exactly what she wanted to do career-wise and what she needed to do to get there. Few of us, I suspect, have this student's drive or organizational acumen, but we nonetheless see in her perspicuity a kind of

ideal in relation to vocation. To discern one's vocational calling is to get as clear-eyed as possible about our gifts, talents
and goals and then envision a path toward their realization.

I want to suggest that this commonplace conception of vocation is not so much wrong as it is incomplete. It takes what
in reality is a relatively rare experience and generalizes it as
normative for the rest of us who don't have our lives planned
out in color-coded spreadsheets. It neglects the ways in which
our context quite often—certainly more often than we would
admit in our more promethean moments—shapes our vocational directions and potentially induces in us an unwarranted
anxiety and even sense of vocational "failure." Some of us are
able to grasp a clear vision of what faithfulness looks like in
our professional and working lives, but many more of us—
and I am certainly in this latter group—either realize along
the way that what they took to be that clear vision was not
that at all or simply "muddle through," attempting to discern
what it means to live faithfully in a context not necessarily of
our own choosing. Sometimes, it seems to me, to fulfill one's
vocation means working out what we are called to do wherever it is we get planted rather than always figuring out how
we can re-plant ourselves elsewhere so as to do what we are
'really supposed to be doing.'

At least, that's the way it has worked out (so far) for me. I
am a political theorist, teaching and writing at an evangelical Christian college in the Midwest. Almost every aspect of
that self-description would be a surprise, even a shock, to
what I planned when I entered graduate school in the fall of
1998 after a stint as an Army intelligence officer. (That job did
not, alas, involve any cloak-and-dagger missions—of course,

that's exactly what you'd expect a spy to say). I first became interested in pursuing a Ph.D. while taking a history seminar entitled "Communism and Its Critics." The experience of reading a book a week and then spending a couple of hours reflecting on its merits and themes was great fun. Indeed, I was rather amazed that institutions might actually pay people to do that. Being a "Modern European Studies" major who focused on communist and post-communist politics in Eastern Europe, it seemed only natural to follow those interests on into graduate school. After a master's degree and then a few years in Army green, I entered my Ph.D. program ready to study and write about post-communist political transitions. More broadly, apropos of my experience in that history seminar, I was keenly interested in understanding how it was that moral values—both good and bad—took hold in public life. Truth be told, these academic interests were driven as much by my then-contemporary concerns about American public values as explanations for post-communist political phenomena. (In what was easily the most surprising element of our reading in that seminar, dissidents such as the Czech playwright, Vaclav Havel, and Polish journalist, Adam Michnik, suggested that the pathologies of Soviet-style communism were not some historical aberration, but instead a horrible exaggeration of philosophical and moral tendencies present in the free societies of the West as well.) In other words, I went into academics because I enjoyed it, was pretty good at it, and because I thought I could contribute to a broader public conversation about our collective moral life.

A funny thing happened, though, on my way to public and academic glory as a scholar of post-communist politics. As a first-year graduate student at Brown, I had to take a seminar in political theory, a subject with which I had only a fleeting acquaintance. (I was such a naïf that I bought a badly edited version of Hobbes's Leviathan and discovered when preparing for class—the night before, naturally—that a few of the assigned chapters had been edited out of my version. They were the ones dealing mostly with religion, of course). It turned out that I loved political theory: I loved its philosophical bent, its attempts to see past the limits of the status quo, and especially its orientation to questions about how we ought to arrange our social and political institutions. Pulling out my theses for my undergraduate and master's degrees, moreover, I realized that I had always already been interested in and in some respects doing political theory. Whether writing about the 1917 Russian Revolution, the Prague Spring, or anti-communist dissident literature, my questions were always about the ideas involved. Why did some ideas take hold and not others? Why would some adopt such obviously bad ideas? I switched subfields and set about learning as much as I could.

The point here is not that what I did was optimal—far from it. One of my intellectual models, Jean Bethke Elshtain, had actually been teaching at Vanderbilt when I was there as an undergrad, but I, lacking the insight and wisdom to understand truly where my gifts and interests lay, don't recall even thinking about taking one of her classes. I expect that I might be a better and more accomplished political theorist had I happened on the discipline earlier in some serious way. Or maybe not. After transferring to Harvard (following my advisor), I wrote a dissertation taking up the question of whether citizenship in liberal polities imposes on citizens an obligation to abstain from employing religious reasons in their political deliberations. Precisely because I had spent so much of my time as a student exploring explanations for empirical political phenomena, I thought I saw something that others had missed about the debate. Namely, I saw that many of the moral arguments made in favor of such abstention had embedded in them some plausible, though far from incontestable, empirical claims, usually predicting all sorts of dire occurrences should citizens or candidates make religiously tinged arguments. I cobbled together a small comparative study of the political effects of religious political parties in late 19th century western Europe and threaded that study's conclusions into my more obviously philosophical claims, attempting to rebut what I called the "liberal consensus." There are plenty (too many, in fact) of books and articles focusing on this normative question, but almost none of them take the trouble to ask empirically-oriented questions and none of them do what my dissertation and first book does, actually try to answer those questions with empirical evidence. I doubt that I would have developed such a work or produced what I think is a pretty good piece of scholarship had I not, in fact, come to political theory "late," as it were.

Sometimes we can see clearly precisely where we ought to be and even the way that leads there. More often, we think we see where we might want to go, but the path is not clear; indeed, often where we think we are going doesn't turn out to be it at all. It is tempting to think of that muddled path with its roundabouts and apparent dead ends as wasted opportunities and lost time. And sometimes it is. But sometimes muddling can be a preparation that allows us to pursue opportunities that would not otherwise have been available to us. Think in this respect of Augustine's Confessions. Augustine tries to do a lot of different things as he looks back over his life, but chief among them is to try to trace out the ways in which his muddling operated within the ambit of God's providential care. We should be careful here, for having confidence in God's providence can sometimes tip over into panglossian naiveté. But we should be just as concerned with its opposite, the despair that all too easily accompanies disappointments or detours. The Confessions should help remind us that we are never lost and that even when we fail or just tread water, those experiences can be redeemed for God's work. So, too, is it with our sense of vocational calling.

I don't mean here to downplay or minimize the very real frustrations, even desperation, that can attend to academic life in particular. I have friends who have spent years pursuing a degree in the full confidence that the scholarly life was indeed their proper calling only to find themselves without a job and feeling hopeless. And if one's vocational aspirations are tied up entirely with the acquisition of a tenure-track job or high-profile publication or academic prestige, it might be right to despair. Though things are not necessarily this way across the board, academia's deep institutional conservatism means that a significant deviation from the "normal" career path—Ph.D., maybe a post-doc, then a tenure-track job—makes it quite unlikely that you will get back on it. (It may sound odd to describe academia as deeply conservative, given most faculties' politically progressive views, but a job candidate with an "odd" or unconventional record is at a significant disadvantage in securing a position). Unless we see things rightly—i.e. through the eyes of faith—such muddling about or what appears to be outright failure can indeed feel devastating, but our attempts to evade such difficulties can be, in some fashion, even worse.

Charles Mathewes' recent book *A Republic of Grace* is helpful in this regard. Mathewes writes in particular about the ways in which Christian participation in public life can be a means of discipleship, of forming us in the virtues of faith, hope, and love as preparation for life eternal. But his framework extends beyond mere politics into most any area of life, including our vocational choices. He suggests that following Augustine helps us recognize ourselves as something other than ex nihilo free actors whose choices are essentially unconditioned. We are agents, to be sure, but we exercise our agency in response to the world and situations we find ourselves in. We are not "masters of our fate" and, yet, we are not the objects of mere fate, either. Negotiating the muddle or even facing failure means recognizing, not that we are powerless, but more to the point that we are, as Christians, inevitably caught up in God's work in the world. This does not insulate us from insecurity, failure, or outright tragedy, but it does mean that such evils are not final and that we may be called (at times) to endure them as opposed to avoiding or overcoming them.

Attending my sister's MFA exhibition, I got the phone call that every Ph.D. so earnestly desires. Pepperdine University, out in Malibu, California, was offering me a tenure-track position. In most every respect, it was a great job: a top-50 university with very good students, collegial and interesting colleagues, and 70-degree February days overlooking the Pacific Ocean. The trouble was that my wife, a neurologist with a good practice in her hometown of Athens, Georgia, was reluctant to move to Southern California. We hemmed and hawed, went back and forth, and finally accepted the position. It turned out to be a mistake, though certainly not because of Pepperdine—they were gracious, accommodating, and I loved my year teaching there. It was a mistake ultimately because we made the decision out of fear, in particular a fear that if I did not accept this position, another one might not be forthcoming and I could see my academic career come crashing down before it really even began. For a variety of reasons, my family stayed in Georgia and I commuted between there and California while we tried to decide whether and how to make the move to California. In the midst of what was really a quite difficult year, I called a friend and asked his advice on what I should do. His question brought me up short. He asked what I thought this position and a move to California for my family meant vis-à-vis the Kingdom of God. How did I think about this in relation to what we might call "Kingdom-work"?

I am sorry to admit that this question had not once even occurred to me. Attending a summer seminar with Nicholas Wolterstorff in 1999, I had become convinced of my responsibility to make myself the best Christian political theorist I could, which at that point meant learning what it is that Christians actually think, e.g. theology. Having grown up in a tradition that did not emphasize explicitly much in the way of theological reflection (as opposed to Scripture), I had a lot to catch up on and had made some reasonable progress in understanding the basics of central theological doctrines and their historical development. What I had not done is to think seriously about how working as a political theorist (and my choices therein) might have Kingdom implications. I don't know for sure that I would have necessarily made a different decision about Pepperdine—it is a great place to teach, after all—but I would certainly have made the decision differently if I had been able to keep clearly in mind the great truth that I am not, ultimately, on my own. Instead, we have been called into this new kingdom in which we can act freely, as it were, without the worry that we are our own masters and, correlatively, support. The fear that drove my Pepperdine decision was premised ultimately on the sense that if I did not take that job that there might not be another one behind it and that if I did not secure a tenure-track job then I would be a failure, full stop. Of course, not securing a tenure-track position would be a failure; there is no need to sugarcoat that. But it is not an ultimate sort of failure. One's life, especially as it relates to the kingdom, is certainly not tied to securing that particular job or really any kind of career advancement—if we can grasp and hold on to that truth, the inevitable disappointments attendant to any vocation can be endured and even turned to our good.

But I want to suggest something even further in regard to thinking about our vocation, especially in the midst of muddle or failure. That is, I want to suggest that it is precisely the experience of landing in unexpected places and doing unexpected things that can, and perhaps should, help "teach" us about our vocation. Think back for a moment to my highly organized college student. Even if we might acknowledge the truth of how we can sustain a commitment to vocation even when we don't see things clearly, we nonetheless probably think that, all things considered, it would be better to have her clarity of vision. Perhaps that is right. But I think that it is probably fair to say that almost none of us (at least those of us with a certain, ahem, maturity) can cast a look back ten years or more and not be a bit amazed at life's twists and turns. Do we ever really have clarity of vision? Or, perhaps more to the point, does our supposed clarity ever work out just as we had planned? I'm rather doubtful. What seems more likely to me is that we are all almost always stuck in that muddle, but that it's not always a bog, a trap for the unwary, but it is in reality a set of opportunities for rethinking and living out our vocation. We might even say that our circumstances, especially the unexpected ones, can be particularly important to our vocational call. Let me illustrate what I mean.

When you teach at a Christian liberal arts college like Wheaton, a few things become quite clear. Chief among these is the fact that the relatively robust teaching load and high expectations students have for faculty interaction leave comparatively less time for research and writing than in other places. It is certainly not impossible to be a highly productive scholar at Wheaton, but the circumstances tilt against it. I will admit that I find that aspect of my position frustrating. I wish I had the time to pursue that list of projects I keep on my computer desktop. But it would be wrong to say that teaching at Wheaton has frustrated what I take to be my vocational call; it has, rather surprisingly to me, transformed it.

There is an old saw that says you write your dissertation for your advisor, your first book for your tenure committee, and then whatever comes next for yourself. That is almost certainly too cynical to be true, but it catches something right, namely, that the circumstances of our positions constrain us in some ways and liberate us in others. At Wheaton, I have of necessity had to think more about and focus more on my teaching, but not just in the sense of trying to communicate to my students the truths (or falsities) of Plato, Locke, and the like. Rather, I have had to think more about my teaching as part of Wheaton's mission to form our students so that they might become "whole and effective Christians." When I lead my students through texts discussing justice, freedom, and virtue, my hope is not just that they will come to understand what those texts' arguments are and develop responses to them, but more that they will use those occasions to develop their own, distinctively and thoroughly Christian responses to them, and in the process become more careful Christian political thinkers themselves. Quite simply on the basis of my circumstances at Wheaton, I have come to understand my vocation as a Christian political theorist as encompassing service to the Church in the form of teaching young Christians how to think well about politics.

I had always understood my vocation to include service to the Church, but I think I imagined it in ways that were, well, a bit more "public." That is, I expected that I could leverage my position and credentials to gain a foothold in public debates and help my fellow Christians be better political actors. It simply did not occur to me while in graduate school to suppose that the "Christian" aspect of my vocation as a political theorist might be most strongly oriented to my teaching. Of course, I planned to mentor and minister to students wherever I ended up, but to have actual classroom teaching be perhaps the most significant thing I do in relation to God's kingdom? It is a deeply discomfiting thought, to tell the truth. Most students pass through my classes generally pleased with our discussions and even the readings. (One student once noted in his evaluation that the class was "extremely hard," but recognized that this was how things ought to be, as he was, in his words, a rather "lazy" student). Occasionally, a student will send a note or indicate in conversation how much a class has meant, and even remark that it sparked some serious rethinking about politics and our faith's orientation toward it. But most simply take that final exam or turn in that final paper and move along. I have no real idea how the class affected them, if it did. What's more, the actual business of teaching is not typically some grand drama of collaborative and joyous intellectual inquiry. It is, like most things, a mixture of occasional successes—like the thirty-five minutes in my political ethics class last fall, when students deliberated with one another in intelligent, civil, and serious ways about whether and how Christians should employ natural law arguments in contemporary public debates—and stretches of steady progress with the inevitable, thankfully relatively rare, complete failure. (I here recall my attempt to explain Hegel while teaching at Pepperdine). Don't get me wrong. I really mostly enjoy teaching, but the thought that it might be, for the moment at least, that to which I am most deeply called vocationally is a little disquieting. It is, frankly, not glamorous or exciting enough and it does not seem to put me in much of a position to help change the world.

I became a Christian the week before Easter as a twelve-year-old boy, walking up the aisle at Pleasantview Baptist Church in Derby, Kansas. On our way out of the service that morning, the pastor said something to my parents that has haunted me ever since: he told them that he was sure that God had prepared me to do "great things" with my life. Great things? Me? What counts as "great"? I know what the broader culture around me counts as great, and it certainly does not include trying to walk students through the complexities of Plato's Republic. It may be enjoyable and even deeply gratifying to participate in students' intellectual and moral development, but there is a reason that nearly every academic satire novel is premised on the gap between the reality of the professor's social and cultural standing and his overblown self-regard.

Even those who are fortunate enough to be significant players in our intellectual fields do not count for all that much in the wider culture; we are not, whatever we might tell ourselves, world-changers. Greatness in that sense seems wildly elusive, or at least greatness in that sense seems wildly elusive for this Christian political theorist teaching at a small Midwestern Christian liberal arts college.

It is tempting, as before, to despair in the face of these kinds of realities—and, indeed, academia has more than its share of scholars who ooze a kind of resentment at the ways the broader culture does not value their (obviously critical) intellectual work. I have felt its lure: if to do something "great" seems out of reach, it is natural, well nigh inevitable, to ascribe the associated frustrations to others, to a "system" out of whack, or the like. Perhaps that is the correct judgment in some cases. It is not so in mine. Rather, I have come to quite a different understanding, helped along by James Davison Hunter's recent book *To Change the World*. There are any number of problems with Hunter's argument—most having to do with his too-simple views regarding the relation of politics and culture—but his call to "faithful presence" helped me see something the world-changer in me had not understood clearly enough. Hunter points out that the dominant frame of Christian engagement in American culture over the past few decades has been one of trying to capture the commanding heights of politics and in so doing be able to leverage power to effect social change. He quite rightly judges those efforts a fairly comprehensive failure, in no small part because it was premised on what he takes to be a sociologically false claim that culture can be leveraged via politics. I tend to think he is a bit too pessimistic on this count, but the broader point he wants to make stands. Christians are tempted to believe that their cultural mission centers on finding and exercising those levers of power within our social order. That is, it centers on being "great" as a means of changing the world.

For some, that is no doubt true, and it would be a profound mistake to suppose that the many Christian failures in cultural and political engagement should be taken as evidence that we should not exercise power when we find ourselves in those positions of authority and influence. Some have taken Hunter's book, probably because he suggests Christians may want to remain silent politically "for a season," as an argument for cultural withdrawal, ala American fundamentalism in the 1920s and 1930s. That is not his argument. Rather, he emphasizes our responsibility in the varied centers of cultural power, but draws a picture of Christians responding to our opportunities as opposed to attempting to seize (or construct) them. There are some delicate nuances to be drawn out here, but at the heart of Hunter's call to "faithful presence" is a model of human agency, indeed a model of Christian vocation, that pulls us away from self-aggrandizing postures of ourselves as ever-possible titans of the world, planning and working to acquire enough power and influence so as to be able to effect our (obviously good) will.

I often tell my students now about my experience in being a teaching assistant for very similar political theory classes at Brown and Harvard. In both classes, students were required to read Aristotle's Politics, which among many other things contains his defense of natural slavery and his views on women's essential irrationality. The Brown students took these errors as reason enough to throw Aristotle to the side entirely. The Harvard students were no more sympathetic to those particular claims, but were not so ready to reject everything, for they liked Aristotle's idea that the virtuous man should rule the city. (They missed Aristotle's ironic worry that a truly good man, say Gary Cooper's character in High Noon, probably could not actually rule). I could see working in the back of their heads the presumption that they, Harvard government students, would indeed one day be our rulers and, of course, they would deserve it on account of their obvious virtue. We are sorely tempted toward being like those Harvard undergraduates, seeing ourselves as obviously virtuous, and mapping out our paths to greatness as a fulfillment of our vocational calling. The deep problem lies not in the fact that some do wield extraordinary power—that seems like an inevitable feature of human societies. Instead, the problem lies in the expectation that fulfilling one's purpose consists in wielding such power and that we should arrange our lives to pursue that goal. In so doing, we suppose that we are capable of seeing how we in particular should be wielding power and we neglect an important, inescapable source of wisdom regarding our vocational call: our experiences and circumstances.

The truth is that we are not in control of where we end up (at least not entirely, maybe not even mostly), and we should reflect seriously on how where we end up ought to shape our vocational vision. Ending up teaching at Wheaton does not mean, I think, that I have failed to take seriously what my vocation as a Christian political theorist means. Rather, to the degree that I think of my time here as standing in the way of what I am supposed to be doing, I am missing my actual vocational call precisely because I have misconceived how I am to discern that call. I have come to recognize as integral to my vocation the obligation to help my students and others I might reach with my teaching develop better ways to think about politics, especially as Christians. But I have come to that recognition not out of some de-contextualized reflective process but instead out of an understanding of where I am and how that situation offers certain opportunities and makes others more difficult. To be faithful in a particular context is, first, to recognize that context for what it is and then ask, given that context, how we might best act with an eye (maybe two!) on what we take to be God's call then and there. This does not simplify our discernment—probably quite the opposite. But I think it avoids the error of believing that a proper understanding of one's vocational call at a particular time emerges out of constructing some clear, final vision for life that all too typically sees current circumstances as mere obstacles to its fulfillment.

There is a delicate balance to be achieved here, for just in the same way that we should not despise our circumstances in thinking about our vocational calls, neither should we be prisoners of those circumstances. We are not simply bound by what we can see in front of us, but, frankly, for many Christians, especially high-achieving ones, the tendency is not to be overly circumscribed in our vocational reflections. We are much more likely to cast our vision in ways analogous to the student I described earlier. Thinking in such ways may indeed at times be helpful in breaking us out of a complacent resignation, but it can just as well cause us to miss the opportunities, even obligations, implicit in our lives as they are. To ignore our circumstances or see them merely as features to be overcome risks missing how those circumstances can become partial tutors in our reflections on vocation. So when I have to set aside my research or writing in order to prepare for class or talk to a student about her paper (or life!), it is possible not to see that as a derogation from what I am supposed to really be doing. For even if I feel the tug of regret (and I do), to not attend to what is right in front of me, what has been brought to me in God's providential wisdom, is to arrogate to myself a power and privilege I do not have. It is also, most importantly, to miss the opportunity to respond faithfully to God's grace both in my own life and in the world at large. It is to miss my vocation.

Full-time Life

Dano Jukanovich
Karisimbi Business Partners
Rwanda

1. Introduction

I was a U.S. Army officer, twenty-six years old and newly married when I applied for graduate schools in anticipation of leaving the Army the next year. I was maybe a typical young, goal-oriented, relatively successful type-A male. I had plans. It's somewhat embarrassing to list, but they included things like getting multiple degrees, becoming fluent in multiple languages, having a net worth of millions of dollars, getting a martial arts black belt, travelling to various countries, climbing mountains, being CEO of a large company, etc., etc., etc. It may not be clear from the above obviously self-absorbed list, but at this time I had been a Christian for more than ten years. Fortunately, God had been at work in me over time, unearthing some well hidden but redeeming interests and character traits.

One of my early memories relates to a fundraising effort that was going on in third or fourth grade. I don't remember the purpose, but I remember being very convicted and compelled to contribute. I took much of what I had saved from allowances over time and gave twenty dollars to the cause.

My earliest leadership experiences were in sports, particularly soccer, but also baseball and football. I played sweeper, catcher and middle line-backer respectively. In all three, I was in some kind of role where I saw all of what was transpiring on the field and then told other people on the team what to do – some things never change.

For as long ago as I can remember, I have had an interest in the world outside the United States, not from a travel and exploration standpoint, but from an international political economic standpoint. The first social science research project I remember doing in school related to World War II and international relations.

When I applied for a Harvey Fellowship for Christian graduate students in 1997, I recognized these innate interests and characteristics and they informed my vision for the future and therefore my application; yet, the vision was certainly still only a work in progress of being unearthed and developed by God. My career goals at the time involved being an advisor to international business and government leaders. I envisioned a job as a senior executive in a multinational or in a consulting or investment banking advisory services firm. There was also a definite faith component to the vision, as I genuinely did want God to use my position of influence to further His kingdom.

Today my wife, my three adopted children – daughters from China and son from Rwanda – and I live in the tiny country of Rwanda, in the heart of the African continent. My two friends and partners and I founded and lead a small socially-motivated consulting and private equity firm called Karisimbi Business Partners whose vision is "to alleviate poverty, improve community, shape industry and inspire others...one business at a time."

At the time of writing this, we've recently returned from advising the new President of Malawi and my partner is in Ethiopia as one of only a six-member Minister-level official delegation from Rwanda representing investment opportunities to participants at the World Economic Forum. In the next two months, my other partner and I are separately off to Nairobi, Washington D.C. and London to speak at conferences, sharing some of our insights with others in the economic development community. It is humbling for me to consider, but in the last three years we have worked with over fifty companies in the East Africa Region and have had a direct role in increasing the incomes and wealth of tens of thousands of rural poor households.

Where I am now is not where I would have planned fifteen years ago, but cliché as it may seem, where I am is much better than what I could have asked for or imagined. God has continued to develop my character and reveal my interests in ways that align with His will and are incredibly fulfilling to me. There has been a popular movement among mid-life successful Christian business people in the U.S. called "half-time." And I reference it in no way disparagingly because it has had enormous positive impact in many peoples' lives for God's purposes. I reference it in comparison to what I'm calling "full-time." God has created us for a full-time, life-long relationship with him that integrates all aspects of who we are, where we live, what we do, and with whom we do it. Full-time as I'm using it here is intended to have a double (or triple) meaning. It references the duration of our lives from childhood to old age. It speaks to the entirety of our beings – physical, emotional, spiritual. And it is a matrix concept wherein what we do, where we do it and with whom we do it overlap with our ideally all-consuming (lifelong and holistic) relationship with God. The remainder of this essay will speak to the evolution of "full-time" in my life, particularly over the last fifteen years and as it relates to vocation.

2. Full-time Theology

Jesus is always and entirely engaged in relationship with his Father. At all times of day and from his earliest days on earth until his last, Jesus was actively and consciously interacting with his Father. When Jesus went missing for three days in the big city at age twelve, his parents were frantic and frustrated. When they finally found him at the temple listening and learning from the teachers there, they demanded an explanation. Jesus answered, "Why were you searching for me? Didn't you know I had to be in my Father's house?"(Luke 2:49)

The Bible follows this scene with a picture of Jesus' adolescent and early adult years as he "grew in wisdom and stature and in favor with God and man"(Luke 2:52). Certainly the Bible is replete with portraits of Jesus' relationship with his Father during the period from when he was baptized in the Jordan until his Ascension. Jesus gives frequent indication that the lifelong aspect of his relationship with the Father is something for all of us, not just Jesus. "Jesus said, 'Let the little children come to me, and do not hinder them, for the kingdom of heaven belongs to such as these'"(Matthew 19:14). The Bible honors the eighty-four-year-old prophetess, Anna, describing her life-long worshiping, fasting and praying in the temple. The story also reveals her blessing Joseph and Mary and the yet-to-be born baby Jesus. He honors the child. He honors the aged. God doesn't just want us "for such a time as this," he wants us always.

Maybe it has something to do with some of my own tenden-cies toward the extreme, but I embrace the fact that God wants us in our entirety. He wants us to be all-in. When Jesus asked Simon and his brother, Andrew, to follow him, they didn't take a moment to consider the pros and cons, but were instead immediately all-in; as the Bible says, "At once they left their nets and followed him"(Mark 1:18). But the idea of being entirely engaged with the Father is not just about these pictures of the fearless, seemingly high-risk decision points in life. While ministering in Galilee, Jesus came upon a man with leprosy who asked Jesus to heal him. Jesus very easily could have stood back and given the command for him to be healed and it would have been done. According to Mosaic Law, Jesus would have defiled himself if he dared touch the man; Jesus did exactly that. Jesus knew that the man's deepest need was not healing, but relationship and he knew that he hadn't been touched by another human being since having been known to have the disease. Jesus was entirely engaged with the man - spiritually, emotionally and physically. That is what God wants of us.

3. Full-time Career

My career to-date has evolved through approximately four five-year cycles: military service, large corporation mid-management, small business ownership, and international economic development. By my early high school years, I was blessed to have developed a genuine interactive relationship with God. I knew God was real and that Jesus was who he said he was. So it was not by some inherent noble character, but only by God's grace, that my career to-date has not been split between an extended attempt to "make it" materially, followed by seeking to do something "meaningful." I can say confidently that one consistent theme throughout various less-than-perfect career decisions has been a genuine seeking of God's will and endeavoring to do what I thought He wanted me to do. It is this career-long seeking of God's will for my vocation that I am referring to as a full-time career.

Deciding to go to the United States Military Academy was really a nine-year commitment – four for college and five for service in the military. That was a significant decision for a seventeen-year-old. There were two reasons I made that commitment: firstly, I knew that God had some design for me related to leadership and that West Point would be a great place to develop that; secondly, West Point felt like a good fit for me vis-à-vis the other options I was considering. In my immature, relatively new-Christian way, I was endeavoring to follow God in this first career choice and it just so happened to align with some of those character traits that God had been developing since I was a seven-year-old on the soccer field.

I also knew that the military was not the place for me for the rest of my life. It was great in almost every way, but I felt there was something more to me than what I would find in the military. Graduate school, after my military service, was really an opportunity for me to transition into what I didn't know at the time. I passionately pursued the opportunity for a Master's Degree in International Relations from Johns Hopkins School of Advanced International Studies (SAIS), but also applied for a simultaneous dual-degree MBA with The Wharton School of the University of Pennsylvania. Finishing this three-year program, the only leading I really felt in my heart and from God was to go back to the Seattle area where I had grown up as a child and where I still had family. The next four years were spent working in corporate finance at AT&T Wireless' Seattle headquarters.

This was the beginning of a time of very serious soul-searching. I had just graduated from a top-tier business school and was earning a great salary. Sure, I was able to put some grand-sounding bullet points on my resume from that time; but for the first two and a half years of this job I was, what I affectionately refer to as, a cubicle-bound Excel jockey. Within about eighteen months, I felt stifled, oppressed, depressed, underutilized, undervalued and whatever other Dilbert-esque pictures one can think of to describe a job situation. There was a phase toward the end of that time in which I spent a fair amount of a given week just trying to get through it. Much of my time was spent comparing myself to co-workers and classmates. I fearfully envisioned myself spending a lifetime as the silent small cog in the wheel of the big corporation. At my lowest points in a given day all I could think to do was to silently sing "Jesus Loves Me" to myself as a reminder that I mattered.

My perspective was by no means entirely attributable to the context, but was in large part derived from my own "issues" that God needed to work out in me and to which I refer later in this essay. Eventually I came to a point in which I told my boss I had to quit or go crazy, and she graciously let me take a six-month quasi-sabbatical where I worked half-time and mostly remotely while spending the other half of my time exploring career options. After this, I came back to the company for another year in a different and much more fulfilling role. In hindsight, this attempt to follow God's leading by choosing to move back to my hometown was fruitful in many ways: as an outstanding vocational training ground, as a way for me to be near my mom for a few years before she passed away and by affording me the mental and emotional space to engage in my own significant spiritual and emotional development.

I resigned from AT&T Wireless the day after it was acquired by Cingular (before being sold back to AT&T); again in an attempt to follow what I believed was God's leading. I pursued different opportunities to lead or own small businesses and ended up becoming a minority owner in a family business, which I proceeded to co-lead for the following five years. Taking on that role was a very clear call from God and, although the most difficult experience of my life, it was also the most rewarding in many ways. What follows is a testimony that my brother and I wrote in late 2006 about our company that summarizes some of what God was doing during that time:

"Through most of 2006, we have focused on and prayed for growth and an opportunity to expand our influence for His Kingdom. It seemed like God answered those prayers almost instantaneously. In early January, we were given an opportunity to partner with one of the largest publicly listed builders to buy and develop a 300-home project. After working tirelessly for almost two months to put together financing and to do feasibility analysis on the project, things fell apart at the eleventh hour. Over the following months, we earnestly sought other similar opportunities. None bore fruit.

Since late 2005, we had been wondering whether we should be more conservative and consider liquidating some assets. We didn't do this. Instead we continued to take on additional debt in order to fuel growth. This fall as the housing market slowed, we realized that we were in over our heads.

We fell to our knees. Over a six-week period, God answered our prayers with a number of messages: "believe in my ability to miraculously provide"(2 Kings 4:1-7); "trust me even if your worst case scenario comes true"(Job 15:13); "you haven't earned my grace, but I give it to you anyway, and it is all you need"(Job 42:1-6); "I won't let you get out of this mess on your own, but instead it will be entirely up to me"(Judges 7).

Over Thanksgiving we spent some time in prayer and acknowledged that what had been driving us over the last year was greed. It was plain and simple greed. It wasn't the flashy "want a new car or big house" kind of greed, but it was the greed that said "we want the success that we see others having." We asked God to forgive us.

On December 2nd, the night of our company Christmas party, we randomly bumped into an interested buyer at a million dollar home we had built. That Monday we walked into the office to a purchase offer from the same man we met Saturday night. He closed on the transaction in eleven days, providing us enough funds to pay subcontractors and employees through January. More amazingly, he was the owner of the 300-lot project we tried to develop twelve months prior. It truly is only by his grace."

Our company no longer exists. Not enough time has passed to really grasp what God did in mine and my family's lives and the lives of those with whom we worked during that time, but I remain convinced that He blessed our less than perfect attempts to follow Him as we led that business.

Today I am in Rwanda continuing to become more of who God has called me to be. The above is only a cursory overview of twenty years that were filled with some very high and very low points from a career satisfaction standpoint. I struggled throughout with pride and insecurity, made significant decisions that were motivated by fear and greed, and spent a fair amount of time generally self-absorbed. But a significant common theme throughout the major decision points was a faithful attempt to discern and follow God's will, often at the exclusion of what was safe and secure. God wants every aspect of our careers to be always (lifelong) and entirely (our whole selves) abandoned to His gracious, life-giving, abundantly, joy-filled and masterful plan.

4. Full-time Spirit

These career transitions happened simultaneously with spiritual transformations. Much of the spiritual transformation happened unbeknownst to me, but in the end required some decisions on my part. The first watershed experience had been building for as long as I can remember.

Success was my God, whether I realized it or not, and regardless of how exactly I defined it. My sophomore year in college I mentored a freshman. This "kid" was on the verge of being kicked out of West Point because he wasn't able to pass a particular physical fitness requirement that was a pre-requisite for moving from freshman to sophomore year. I was with him at the gymnasium where he was starting to sound suicidal and opening up about how West Point meant everything to him and how it would allow him to finally earn some respect among his peers and family back home and how he couldn't go home and face them if he didn't graduate. I came back to my dorm and relayed the conversation and experience to a close friend of mine. At one point I said to her that "the kid just needs somebody who cares about him for who he is, not for what he does or how he performs." She responded that it "sounds like somebody else I know."

That was a Holy Spirit-inspired moment because I immediately broke down in tears, recognizing the truth in what she said about my own brokenness. By His grace I recognized this as stemming from God's relentless pursuit of me. For whatever reason, I could not go back to what I had perceived as "living" before this experience. I am forever grateful for that moment. It wasn't immediate but in that instant God transformed me in my spirit. I practically spent more time enjoying life and less time striving for "success" after that. I spent more time serving and caring for my classmates. I spent more time with the kids that we were leading in the local Young Life club. It may sound a little dramatic, but "amazing grace, how sweet the sound that saved a wretch like me."

The next thick layer of the onion hiding who I really was came off during my early 30s (supposed to happen in one's 20s, but I was a little behind). One evening, sitting on the front steps of our house in Seattle, I said to my wife, "I really don't know who I am." More specifically, I said, "I don't know where my parents' or friends' or society's expectations of who I'm supposed to be stop and where who I really am starts." I made a decision at that point that I was not going to stay in that same place of ignorance any longer than I absolutely had to. I spent a fair amount of time over the next couple years seeking counsel from spiritual directors and friends. Through that process, I came to realize that it was through knowing God's love that I would be free of trying to find fulfillment in meeting my own or others' expectations of who I should be.

A fair amount of this process involved, in particular, choosing to no longer hold my parents or my wife accountable for fulfilling a role that only God was capable of fulfilling. Pardon me for preaching for a moment, but insofar as we are looking for God in something or somebody other than God, we are destined for disappointment. And our natural inclination from birth is to look for God in those we love and whom we believe should love us unconditionally. At some point we all have to go through a transaction in which we recognize that we have been let down by those whom God intended to love us unconditionally. Then we have to accept that Jesus is the only one capable of filling that role and that He has done so perfectly and self-sacrificially. On the other side of that process, we can move forward with developing a life inspired

with the peace, joy and confidence that comes from genuinely knowing we are loved unconditionally. Again thanks be
to God for His tireless and lifelong pursuit of our spiritual
transformation.

A more recent come-to-Jesus encounter is reflected in my
coming to believe in a few concepts I had never subscribed
to in over twenty years of being a Christian: "God is good,
all the time;" "By His grace alone;" and "Though he slay me,
yet I will praise him." Maybe it stemmed from growing up
with my mom who could not walk and wondered why God
allowed her life to be so difficult, but I definitely spent much
of my Christian life indulging the question of 'why does God
let bad things happen to good people?' Then in 2008 my
family travelled to East Africa as part of a trip sponsored by
an orphan-care organization where my wife was a board
member.

The bone-crushing poverty of the child-headed household we
saw in Northern Uganda on that trip used to be the case study
for me regarding why God was not good all the time. God had
been working in my heart over recent months and years such
that I was ready to see this from a different angle. Reading
Gary Haugen's book, *Just Courage: God's Great Expedition
for the Restless Christian*, was part of the process. Being tired
of hearing people, including myself, say, "but what can we
do?" was part of the process. When we left that village and
got back to our church, I saw a group of people mobilize from
a world away to help the kids in this one village whom they
had never met. This became the case study for me illustrating
why God is good all the time.

During the time depicted in the earlier testimony about our family business, at one point my incredibly gracious wife grew tired of my wallowing and she challenged me to read the last part of Job. The part that spoke to me was where Job recognized that he had been arrogant in thinking that he did not deserve any of the troubles that had been visited upon him. After a direct confrontation with God, Job recognized that he was wrong in trying to call God to account. Instead Job concluded, "Surely I spoke of things I did not understand, things too wonderful for me to know…I despise myself and repent in dust and ashes." I realized the same. I had been accusing God of not coming through for me. I did not trust God because he had "failed to perform" in the past. And I also realized, as did Job, that it was only by God's grace that we walk, and talk and have our being. This was another first for me. I had always struggled with people who so tritely gave "all the glory to God," because it didn't seem sincere. That was because I had never said it with sincerity. But having no explanation other than God's grace left me with no one else to whom I could attribute the glory.

The most painful conversion was for me to get to a point in which I could say, "though he slay me, yet I will praise him." Sitting at the foot of your sleeping daughter's bed full of fear, crying and praying that you'll be able to continue to pay for her pre-school and keep the house that she is living in brings you to a point of decision. Maybe it's our sinful nature that requires us to go to some kind of spiritually dark place before we're able to make the commitment. Fortunately I didn't choose the alternative path that I feel might have led to a permanent renouncing of my faith. I'm not sure but I think the alternative to praising him in the midst of being slain is to curse him. Prior to that decision point, I had just avoided the question, but I'm glad I was faced with the decision and chose to praise him. God wants our hearts in their entirety and he wants them all the time. I am so glad He is gently, yet skillfully, remaking us in His image.

5. Full-time Community

I had never before considered the magic of a three-party partnership until I had the opportunity to enjoy one. When there are three, two can be at odds and the third can mediate. With three there are more perspectives and more gifts and talents to go around. Three people share the load and share the wealth instead of two. It's more fun to get together with three people. Karisimbi Business Partners has three partners and it is so much better than any partnership I have had in the past where there were only two. I won't theologize about the trinity because I don't know if it applies, but in the future I will seek out partnership opportunities where there are more than two parties. We came to Rwanda with a ready-made community, having moved here together as three families. Little did we know how divinely inspired that plan was. It is enough to say that we have been family to each other through these years.

We had the good fortune of facing some major relational hurdles prior to our moving to Rwanda and then immediately upon our arrival. These had to do with embracing each other's differences. They included significant discussions about finances. We worked through partnership agreements to include details of how much we expected of each other in terms of hours worked and vacation time. Our first, fundamental philosophical disagreement came within a month of our arrival in Rwanda. We were at odds about what two of us perceived as fundamentally an integrity issue, which related to our Christian values. As with any partnership, be it a marriage, a friendship or a business partnership, what ended up winning out was the relationship and our commitment to maintaining the relationship above really any other differences. It is that commitment that has held our partnership together through what at times is an incredibly challenging environment for relationships.

Speaking with credibility as an introvert, I believe nothing good happens alone. That's not entirely true, but it's certainly true that so much good happens in community. Looking back on life, I'm sure we can all see those individuals and groups of people whom God used to shape and mold us, whether we knew it or not at the time. What's more interesting to consider is how we have engaged with our communities throughout our lives. The impact of those communities on us has been directly and probably exponentially proportionate to how much we have engaged.

I have to highlight my family's time in Seattle and at Rainier Avenue Church from 2001 to 2009 as one of these seasons of community engagement. My wife and I lived within five minutes' drive of the church. This was an intentional move based on how God had been speaking to us in regard to the value of living and worshiping among those who differ from us. We served on the board of directors. At various times we were actually employed by the church in part-time or project-based capacities. I got to help lead a project to remodel the 100-year-old church building. Jennifer had the chance to create a philosophy for Children's Ministry and see it implemented. Our friendships throughout inner-city Seattle ran deep and wide. We built relationships with over fifty young people in our neighborhood who participated in a weekly summer barbeque at our house. We walked with them as they played, laughed, fought and as two of them died. Our friends loved us as we struggled with infertility. My neighbor became my best friend with whom I still talk almost weekly from Africa. There was the 30-something co-ed soccer team, the Seattle-to-Portland bike ride crew, mommy's group, and the guys' group hikes in the Cascade Mountains. My pastor challenged me to take risks and be faithful. My friends challenged me to face my demons. We were fully engaged for eight years in the same neighborhood and the same church and with the same friends. That community was the highlight of that life-season, far outshining anything vocationally. This was a glimpse into living in community in a complete and consistent full-time way.

6. Full-time Life

Full-time theology, career, spirit, community and life are not references to the hours of the day but to the longevity and the extent of our engagement with God in all areas of our lives. The duration of the relationship God desires is life-long and the extent of the relationship is complete. Though we may, God will stop at nothing less.

Late summer 2008, I distinctly remember walking through the streets of Queen Anne Hill on a beautiful Seattle summer day. I had just left the office of a business advisor. While walking back to my car I made the decision that within the next twelve months I would move to the developing world and actively engage in a way that would directly honor the poor, the widow and the orphan. In the summer of 2009 we moved to Rwanda and started Karisimbi Business Partners.

In between those two dates, a lot happened. We spent three weeks visiting orphan-related ministries in East Africa and fell in love with Rwanda. We almost went to work for a large NGO in Rwanda. After that opportunity failed to materialize, we spent a weekend with our good friends, Carter and Kerry Crockett, and birthed the idea that would become Karisimbi Partners. We (mostly Carter) spent hours upon hours doing research, praying, and analyzing what we might be able to do in a place like Rwanda. We travelled back and forth to Rwanda multiple times. Our friends, the Urquharts, decided to not only generously support Karisimbi Partners, but to join as one of the founding Partners. Throughout that summer of 2009, our families all landed in Rwanda at various times and began to build lives here.

Since arriving here a lot has happened. Most importantly we have two additions to our families: our two-year-old adopted son, Nathanael, and the Urquhart's five-year-old adopted son Marcel. Our wives and children have thrived in this environment. We have been very fulfilled in our work and we know God has used us. We have no idea what the future holds. But I know that where I am today feels like a natural evolution and I expect the next phase of life will also.

Leading, defending the defenseless, and loving the people of the world are parts of who I am. God has developed in and revealed that to me from my earliest days. My career to-date has been marked by decisions to follow what I believed at the time God wanted me to do. Whether as a melancholy middle-school kid or a thirty-year-old in search of an identity, God was pursuing me and transforming my heart. And none of the last forty years happened outside of community. God is a full-time God and he wants us to live a full-time life. He wants all of who we are and he wants us all the time.

Integrating Faith and Vocation in a Research Career

David E. Lewis
Vanderbilt University
Nashville, TN
USA

1. Introduction

I see many things differently now than I did before I started in earnest on the path to becoming a professor at a research university. I did not know any professors that were Christians in my field when I began on this path. I did, however, have the benefit of observing some Christian professors in other fields.

In writing this I have tried to think about what I wish I had known when I started on this journey. Some of what I know now, I knew then. For example, I knew that being faithful is more important than being successful and is the only real measure of success. I knew that God cares about me and knows me intimately. And, while I know it better now than I did then, I knew that God is good.

That said, I know more now about integrating faith and vocation than I did earlier in my career. What I have to relay here comes from experience more than careful theological study and should be read as such. Others have thought more carefully and reliably about the integration of faith and vocation. My hope in laying out my own experience is that it provides readers something to learn from, react against, or strive for as God leads.

A couple of themes emerge. First, there is some perfectly understandable and expected uncertainty about how to integrate faith and vocation. We may have clear pictures in our heads, what we sometimes call vision, but these pictures are often not what God has called us to. Part of the joy inherent in a life of faith is seeing how God's love reflected through us manifests itself in our vocations in different but wholly godly and beautiful ways. Second, integrating God into a research career is not always straightforward, particularly for those of us working in non-normative fields. I have found some practical ways of integrating God into both the process but also the substance of research.

2. Faithful in Uncertainty

It is normal for a person to be unsure about how to integrate their faith and vocation. Indeed, some persons are not attached to one vocation and sometimes vocation is too strong a word for what we do to earn a living. Our drive for certainty and for a vision drives us to rely on pictures in our heads about what our life and work should look like. Most of us entering professions as Christians have a picture in our heads about what that looks like. This can be the picture of the Christian businessperson,

mother, athlete, or scholar. These pictures are defined and rein-
forced in books and illustrated by prominent examples.

Some of these pictures can be useful heuristics or encouraging models but many are, unfortunately, limiting. The truth is
that those of us trying to integrate faith and vocation have to
live with some measure of uncertainty. It may not be entirely
clear to us how our faith and work connect; and, when our
lives do not look like what we envisioned, this can lead to
confusion and doubt. While it is a God-given responsibility
to search out how to integrate our faith and vocation, our
efforts to do so may only bear fruit over time and as a result
of faithful searching. Our primary call is to be faithful and,
through this faithfulness, to let God transform us into his vision of what it means to be a Christian in our current context.

God can and does push us in the direction he wants us to go
through the example of his work by others in our fields, but
it would be surprising if he created us to all look the same
and be gifted in the same ways. Studying the lives of Christian
academics before me and becoming acquainted with other
Christian professors has been very helpful to me, but it can
only take me so far in figuring out how to integrate my faith
and vocation. In fact, part of walking faithfully with Christ
is dealing with uncertainty. I have lived for a long time in
academia, not knowing exactly how to integrate my faith and
vocation, only figuring it out in bits and pieces over time.
When I was in graduate school I thought this was frustrating.
Now I think that uncertainty might be a gift.

Most of us entering professions as Christians have a picture in
our heads about what that looks like. Some aspects of these

pictures are fuzzy and others clear. I kept bumping up against a particular vision of what a Christian professor looks like, and I never comfortably looked like that person. As a young graduate student I had vague optimistic notions about how much I could accomplish for God as a professor. I imagined talking about Jesus in my classes and writing important treatises that would advance God's kingdom on Earth. I assumed there were specific topics that I would cover as a Christian. I thought a Christian in political science would be concerned day to day about the status of faith in the public sphere or argue for the need for righteous policy-making so that God's judgment would not fall on the United States. These activities, combined with an amazing pedagogy completed my fuzzy picture of what a Christian professor would look like. I envisioned something like the fictional Mr. Chips, the inspiring educator dedicated to his students, who continues to impart soul-filling humanity and values in addition to knowledge.

Many of my family members and parishioners share this view of what a Christian professor should be. Staff workers with campus ministries propose book studies on the recent works covering these topics and discuss them with faculty over coffee. Different groups on campus approach Christian faculty to sign petitions and attend public events to add gravitas to their efforts. The idealized Christian professor is at the forefront of larger public efforts to advance God's Kingdom on Earth, however that is conceived. It is often conceived in political or social terms such as marriage, sanctity of life, sexuality, or religious freedom.

Many Christians in political science that I know fit comfortably into these categories. I have treasured and talented colleagues who are spending their careers thinking deeply and writing about the role of faith in a democracy. They are doing so better than I ever could. They care deeply about their students and faithfully spend hours preparing classes and grading student papers. I have other colleagues who see it as their role to publicly defend the faith as they understand it in writing, speaking, and media appearances. God bless them. This seems to be what they were created for. Every issue of faith in the public sphere, every moral issue, they are happy to talk about and articulate views about.

I have not become the Christian professor that a younger me envisioned. There are a couple of reasons for this. First, I was not particularly good at answering the questions I thought Christian professors should be interested in. When I first entered graduate school I entered as a political theorist. I wanted to be a C.S. Lewis or Francis Schaeffer, consistent with the vision I described above. I read political thinkers from Aristotle to Rawls. About two years into my graduate program my advisor asked me why I was studying political theory, the implication being that I was not particularly good at it. I worked very hard but I had little talent. It turns out I was better at estimating statistical models and studying contemporary American politics than thinking deep thoughts about the role of faith in the public sphere.

Second, I am significantly more interested and passionate about other questions that have nothing to do with these issues. I ended up studying the U.S. presidency, largely because I felt there was important work to do on the topic. There was a lot I did not know and, I thought, a lot that others did not know either. The further I got into graduate school, the more I became interested in the Executive Branch more broadly. The bureaucracy is a topic most find dull and incomprehensible, but I wanted to find out how bureaucracies got created, designed, and how presidents control them or do not control them. And I wanted to get it right, which required learning lots of arcane details about the fifteen cabinet departments and fifty-five to sixty independent agencies that define the administrative structure of the U.S. government. When I began down this research path I had no idea how this topic connected to my faith. When people tried to push me to figure out how what I studied was integrated into my relationship with Jesus, I could explain how my faith influenced how I did my work (e.g., good work ethic, graciousness, care in research, etc.) but grew frustrated when people pushed me to explain how the topic of my research was connected to my faith. The honest answer at that time was that I did not know but that I loved studying what I was studying.

The natural process of following what interested me and following Christ has led me to a place where my faith and research are easier to connect. Over time, my research has gained more of an overarching redemptive coherence but this was not a product of forethought. I believe now that God's purpose in this world is to redeem its culture, structures and institutions, along with its people. Among the most important institutions are governmental institutions. Trying to make transparent what government institutions do and why provides a means, ultimately, of figuring out ways of making them work better. Governments exist to provide justice and help us solve problems collectively. Figuring out how to make government agencies work effectively and fairly is incredibly important. Redemptive institutions work more like they would in a world not suffering under the fall. By making transparent how these bureaucracies work and what makes them perform differently in distinct circumstances, I hope I can contribute to making them work a little better to serve the people they were created to serve. In some small way I can help the world look a bit more like God would have it look.

What about Mr. Chips? Surely, the Christian professor has students over to the home and has a life-giving, transformative effect on students through dedicated attention, careful reading of student papers, and long hours of consultation during office hours. The truth is that I was trained in and have spent most of my time working in research universities. Research universities reward faculty for activities related to research. To get promoted in this environment requires conducting research that is recognized according to professional standards. Most faculty I know well work extraordinarily hard at their research because they must in order to do their job well and because they want to intrinsically. The time spent on research competes with time preparing for class and mentoring students, not to mention university service and all of the things God calls us to in our families, churches, neighborhoods, and the world. For most of my career I have lived with the uncomfortable knowledge that I have not done all I could with my teaching and with the sense that I have given my all and still fallen short of what I had hoped to achieve.

I have not surveyed my colleagues but I suspect that many of us regularly experience guilt associated with not giving as much as we would like to teaching and mentoring or parenting and family relationships, for that matter. Most of us feel worse about our performance as parents, caregivers, housekeepers, friends, and sons and daughters than we want known. We know it and try to push it down and keep plowing ahead. I suspect most of us have sacrificed time thinking about and engaging in these things for our research. Few of us have or live out a clear theology of pedagogy except to say that our pedagogy, like our research, has to be integrated into a life defined by the goal of walking with Jesus and serving him. As much as we enjoy teaching and want and should do it well, we love research and treasure time away from the concerns of teaching to conduct research. Some of us really look like Mr. or Ms. Chips but most of us only look like this professorial vision in our best moments.

Does the fact that I look different than what I and others envision(ed) imply that I am not following Christ faithfully? Honestly, sometimes I wonder. This is partly because I recognize my own weaknesses. Most of us writing chapters for this volume could fill it with shameful shortcomings that should surely disqualify us for speaking about what it means to follow Christ in any circumstance. There are the times when we are ashamed or at least hesitant to identify with Christ in the company of colleagues. It is rarely cool to be a Christian in a secular university setting. Sometimes that label characterizes you as an oddity. In other cases, it characterizes you as a bigot or an idiot or scheming conservative. Each new job or position or relationship means letting people know all over again that you follow Jesus. I do not find those interactions easy, as cleansing and healthy as they are. In other cases I do not want to be named with Christ for his sake. Surely, if people associate Christ with my arrogant pronouncements, petty behavior or angry outbursts, Christ is better off not being connected with me. These shortcomings make me wonder if I might look more like the good Christian Professor Chips if I were walking more closely with Christ.

I also question what I have become because of how frequently I bump up against the vision of the Christian professor that I describe above. You cannot help but feel the silent confusion and disappointment when Christians find out that you are a professor and you do not meet their expectations. Some of this has to do with the fact that most people do not understand what research professors do. But, some of it has to do with the, "if I had a platform like you have, I would do this and that" mentality. I cannot blame them. I think too little about how to advance God's kingdom and purposes on my campus, in my neighborhood, and in my community. I would like to see for myself what a life completely sold out for Christ looks like in my position and how this would influence my students, colleagues, neighborhood, and city.

I am fairly certain, however, that if Christian faculty lived lives fully embodying Christ, in many cases it would look dramatically different than the images we and others carry around in our heads. The image of the Christian professor is incredibly limiting and inconsistent with my experience and my understanding of God. A person filled with God's love looks dramatically different than other people (even Christians) and in diverse and unexpected ways. Yes, there are marks we recognize but they spill out through the prism of our unique personal design in odd and wonderful ways. Spend time with people in art, film, rock bands, hedge funds, furniture design, and even ministry; and authentic Christ followers are beautifully and wonderfully diverse and unexpected. Sure, we identify openly with Christ and share his love with those around us in word and deed—but in lovely, godly, and unique ways.

One of my closest friends is a chemistry professor at a major research university. He is a wonderfully gracious and close friend and an extraordinary chemist. There is little in this world that he loves more than chemistry. You know what? I think God made him this way. I would hate to have him be something different than he is, to spend his time on television or leading some movement. Does he try to follow Christ faithfully? Yes. Does he belong to and participate in the work of Christ in his local church? Yes. Does he spend an inordinate amount of time thinking about and working on chemistry? Yes. It is a passion. Can this passion interfere with his following Jesus? Yes. Most of us who are passionate about what we do can relate. Our passions often compete with Jesus for our affections and we wrestle with this all of our lives. From the outside, however, I see that he is who God made him to be. God gets pleasure out of seeing His love lived out in my friend's life, not only in my friend's relationships and church work but in his faithful pursuit of his research and all that this pursuit entails. God calls people to be his own from all over the world, from low and high positions, with different jobs, and they're all broken. It would be strange, indeed, if all of the people he called from this diversity looked the same and fit our finite created visions for what they should look like.

I cannot say for certain that God has not called me to be the person I imagined when I was twenty-two, but I am pretty sure. I do not know exactly what God wants me to look like now but he is showing me slowly and patiently. I am hopeful that faithfully following Christ will transform me into what he wants me to be, something quite different and perhaps fuller and more beautiful than what I envisaged.

3. Redeeming Research

One of the distinctive features of a research career is that our work is defined by discovery and writing. It is not immediately clear what influence faith should have on research and writing. Sure, there are general principles that most agree should characterize research by Christians. Some of these principles are easy to understand and anticipate in advance because they apply to other types of work and usually conform to professional norms. Others become clear through experience and observation. What is also true is that it is often easier to think about how to integrate faith and vocation in terms of process rather than substance. The harder question for many of us is whether what you study is influenced by your faith, rather than just how you study.

3.1 The Process of Research: Integrity

There are general principles that guide the research process. Most of us would agree that research should be careful, honest, transparent and well-crafted. Our desire to please God should be reflected in the way we do research. It should be publicly defensible and conducted to the highest professional standards. In other words, if someone had been watching over our shoulders throughout the process, they would understand and find appropriate the choices made. If our research were replicated and given a full public hearing we would not be embarrassed by our laxity or the way we interpreted the data we uncovered to support one view or another.

On the contrary, even what is not on public display should be excellent. When we dig deeper into God and his work, we never find anything shabby. It is good through and through. Similarly, our research product should be the result of persons who take craftsmanship seriously. We are disappointed when we purchase a product and find substandard materials or work below the surface. I think this a God-given impulse. Most of us would agree that there should be more behind the counter than is on display, both in our lives and in our research.

In the context of my research into politics, this is a pretty demanding standard. Writing these words makes me wince. I have not consistently lived up to this standard. To hold myself to it I try to set up processes and practices in advance that increase the chances that my research will achieve these standards. For example, I try to make all of my data and analysis publicly available for replication and stick as close to the data as I can when I make conclusions. I also try to set up a process in advance that lets others in as the research develops so that it is done in a semi-public way all along.

Those steps have helped a lot and been an important check. They have also, I believe, improved my research. Research that tells us something durable or true about our world will last. These steps I have built in to my research, however, are not fail-safes. There are challenging personal choices all along the way regarding emphasis and interpretation. The best we can do sometimes is develop a practice of asking ourselves questions like,

Why I am doing this research this way?

Is this a defensible choice?

Is God, who knows my heart, pleased with these hidden choices?

Do I have anything to be ashamed of?

Integrating our faith into our research means conducting our research with integrity both in the common way of not lying, fabricating data, or stealing but also in deeper ways associated with the fact that you likely will know more than anyone else on a particular subject and this can give you power. Integrity influences how you treat that fact in your research. Do you use it as power to be protected, in order to manipulate outcomes in your favor? Or, do you make transparent what you know and how you know it, to invite others to join you when you can and, in other cases, treat your privileged position respectfully and humbly before God?

The preceding paragraphs could be summed up in the common sense and widely accepted admonition that research should be conducted with integrity. To label this precept as common sense does not imply that it is trite or easy. It requires tremendous fortitude, humility, and trust. It requires fortitude because doing work well usually requires serious and grinding labor. Extra work has to be put in beyond what might be sufficient for publication. Humility is demanded because doing work well requires the willingness to be proven wrong and often to be transparent in a way that reveals our shortcomings and lack of knowledge. Real research in my field is not searching for evidence that proves my theories or preconceived ideas (i.e., confirmation bias) but evidence that either verifies or falsifies previously held (and published) views. The best research often emerges from a process in which others are allowed in to comment, advise, and critique. This can be incredibly humbling. In a field where intelligence or cleverness is the most important virtue, revealing what you lack through presenting vulnerable work is incredibly risky and humbling, but also godly. A healthy trust is necessary because there are risks to doing careful work and making your work and its shortcomings transparent. Can God overcome the risks that I am taking? Do I want to reveal that I am not that smart? What if it costs me publication, a job offer, or tenure?

3.2 The Process of Research: Respect for Interlocutors

Another, perhaps less obvious way of integrating faith into a research vocation is to let it influence how we treat our interlocutors in speaking and in our writing. Jesus names among the greatest commandments that we love our neighbors as ourselves (Mark 12:31). A defining characteristic of the Christian is that the love of Christ emanates and spills out from the person. When Christ changes us--demonstrates his love for us--we cannot help but be changed and share that love with the people around us. The people around us include our fellow travelers in the profession.

What does it mean to love our colleagues in the profession? There are lots of possible answers to this question but let me highlight three things. First, it simply means recognizing what our colleagues have done. The game of publication requires proving that what we are doing is important. An important component of that is to demonstrate that existing work does not address appropriately the question being asked. What can distinguish a godly character from a less godly character is the way we treat those writing and doing research in our areas. This means careful review of the literature and resisting the temptation to avoid citing certain work. What can distinguish godly work in part is that its review of existing work lacks self-serving mischaracterizations of existing research written to make your work look more important. Indeed, there is a strong temptation to characterize existing work in the most limited or least charitable light to sharpen the contrasts that will clarify the new contribution.

In the headlong rush of research and the joy of discovery we often happen onto ideas or data before we have figured out what others have done before us. It is easy in these contexts to push quickly for publication, particularly if the ideas are good and the discovery is important or time sensitive. In our pushing forward, a careful and gracious treatment of the existing literature can be sacrificed. Two examples will suffice. In the first case, I completed a manuscript on presidential appointments. The last stages of the writing involved a detailed case study and large-N data analysis. In the early stages of the research I had read most everything I could find on the specific aspect of presidential appointments I was evaluating but had put off reading more broadly until later. Unfortunately, later never came. When the press was putting the manuscript together they suggested a new title that was clearer and more general. I accepted their recommendation without too much thought. I realized to my dismay a few weeks later that the book title they suggested was almost exactly the same title as a book on the same general topic published in 1981 (which I had not cited). This led to awkward apologies from me to the author of the original book but it was hard to undo what had been done and it did Christ little credit.

In the second case, two colleagues and I stumbled across some interesting new data that applied to an old and important question. This new data would allow us to make claims that we thought were new and would have had been hard to test before. We wrote the paper relatively quickly to present at a conference that was coming up soon. Our general sense was that we understood the literature in this area and we wrote the literature review and set-up with less care than we should have. A friend and colleague was at the conference who had written two or three pieces that made the same argument we were making and that we had not cited. This was not just careless, it was hurtful and something I hope not to repeat.

These two examples illustrate the larger point that integrating faith and vocation requires taking Jesus' command to love others as ourselves seriously. Our obligation is to carefully consider the work done by others, read it carefully, and represent it accurately in our work.

A second way to love our colleagues is to share credit where it is due. Scholarship is a collaborative endeavor but accolades are frequently given out individually. This creates the incentive to leave people with the impression through your silence that you are mainly responsible for joint work. The majority of my good ideas have come from colleagues. These are ideas they suggested and I took them and executed them, but the ideas still were generated by someone else. Where I can I have publicly and in print acknowledged that the original idea was theirs. This costs me something in esteem but more accurately reflects Christ's character.

A final way to love your colleagues is through the way you engage their work in seminars or in written form. Researchers are judged according to intelligence. When a group of political scientists are together, they evaluate each other primarily through the cleverness of what is spoken or written. A common way that academics demonstrate their intelligence is by insightful comments in seminars or careful critiques in journal reviews. Scholars like to demonstrate their own value or worth through their ability to find hidden weaknesses in others' work by referencing a logical or statistical flaw or set of works or facts that the author has missed. One virtue I have learned over the course of my career, particularly from one specific colleague, is that what really distinguishes the good from the clever is the motive of critique. This colleague, almost without fail, provides critiques that are given with the interest of the author rather than the critic in mind. His comments are regularly brilliant and are always intended honestly to be helpful. He does not need to prove he is smart and this frees him up to be a really generous interlocutor. His comments are given at the level of the author or speaker. When the speaker is a scholar whose work is problematic he does not blast them with devastating critique beyond what they could conceivably do. Rather, he gently pushes them in a direction that will allow them to salvage something out of an otherwise not very promising project.

This has been a real challenge to me. So often, I sit in seminars trying to think of something smart to say, not because I care about the speaker and their project but because I want to demonstrate to my colleagues my own intelligence. Similarly, when I review articles for journals my posture is often impatience or irritation if I have been asked to review a piece I think is poor.

One way to love my colleagues is to be silent when my motivation is to glorify myself. I can love them also by putting myself in their shoes and try to help them be the best political scientist they can be. In reviews I can take this approach as well. At my best, I spend as much time as I can discussing the good things in a paper and praising the author. When I critique, I try to suggest ways around my critique or of fixing the problem. When I find shortcomings I try to decide whether the shortcomings are serious. In many cases papers or projects may not be redeemable. If this is the case I try to patiently and gently describe why and suggest possible alternate or related tacks to take. Research is a tough profession, with more bad news than good. One way to love our colleagues is to engage our colleagues' work in a helpful and sympathetic but truthful way. We can follow the admonition to speak the truth in love rather than just speak the truth (Eph 4:15).

3.3 The Substance of Research

When I was first confronted with questions about how to integrate my faith and vocation, I thought more about process than about substance. I could not see how my research into the design of bureaucratic agencies had any connection to my faith. This was a view shared by many of my Christian colleagues in research fields such as chemistry or neuroscience. When we thought of connecting our faith to our vocation we were limited to the process of our research. The longer I have worked in political science, however, the more connections I see between my faith and the content of my research. This is not to say that I have turned back to the image of research that I had as a younger person. I have not moved away from what naturally interested me to the topics that I once thought

I should be studying. Rather, God has shown me ways of involving him in my choice of topics and the construction of research.

As I explained above, my research has gained a redemptive coherence which I have only recently realized. I am skeptical about whether my colleagues who research topics in math or chemistry will find their research topics coming together in the same way. This does not imply, however, that the substance of what we study is somehow divorced from our lives as followers of Jesus. This came to my attention as a young professor working to get tenure at Princeton. My practice up to that point had been to follow interesting topics and ask God for blessing as I tried to conduct research and get it published. The prayers usually were of the "please help me!" variety. I would ask God to help me do what needed to be done. If I did not get publications I was going to have real trouble (i.e., public embarrassment, loss of a job, etc.).

After my first book, it was time to turn to a second project which was going to be necessary for a realistic shot at tenure. I was considering two topics prior to my sabbatical. I was equally interested in both topics and I thought I might be able to make a contribution in either one. It was a huge decision from the standpoint of my career. I realized, given the magnitude of the decision, that this was a decision I should pray about and ask God for guidance. This is the first time I can remember asking God what I should study rather than for the help to do well what I had already chosen to do. Asking God to help me choose what to do was an important step in breaking down the tension between my career ambitions and my faith. These two loves were often in competition with each other. Asking God to help me choose what to do and trying to listen was a conscious and symbolic submitting of this passion to God's direction.

In retrospect, God blessed this decision. I cannot observe what would have happened with the other project but I am persuaded that I chose the better of the two topics. How do I know? I base this conclusion partly on professional judgment in retrospect. I chose the bigger and more important topic. I also base it partly on small encouragements and private assurances that we receive in our faith life along the way. Notably, I do not think one topic was more godly or more worthy than the other.

This raises an interesting question in the integration of faith and research. Are there some topics that are inherently better than others? The answer has to be yes but perhaps not in the way we normally think of it. I am not going to venture into the appropriateness of research into the profane, etc. Rather, there are subtle differences between research topics that influence their worthiness.

Each of us in research is rewarded based upon what we produce. Very smart and gifted researchers are denied reappointment, funding, or tenure because of a lack of productivity. Raises and professional esteem are determined by our record of publication and grants. This creates goal displacement in academia where the goal becomes publication rather than the research itself. Some of our colleagues are fully given over to this cynicism and happy to publish works for the sake of publication. Others, however, are more resistant, working and trying to conduct research that will have a lasting impact.

I am inclined toward the latter approach. This is not to say that small, incremental advances are not worth publishing and we do not always know what are small or big ideas in advance. Rather, many of us know what publications are really "inside baseball" targeted at small debates going nowhere and we also know that some manuscripts can be published but do not do enough or are not deep enough to make an impact. If our primary reason for selecting a topic for a paper is to get published or to be clever, we may want to reevaluate.

There is another way that my faith and the substance of my research connected in unexpected ways. In the midst of my desperation to finish my second manuscript I began to understand more deeply how to integrate faith and vocation by inviting God into the research in a macro way but also day to day. In the fall of 2006 I had what I thought was a complete book manuscript. I had shopped it to presses and had two interested. Even so, I decided to solicit additional feedback on the manuscript. Scholars critiquing the manuscript agreed that I needed at least one more chapter and some revision of the existing chapters. I had a deadline from the press I had chosen at the end of March. The period from the late fall through March was one of the most difficult of my life as I wrote a new and complete chapter and completely revised the manuscript.

At the start of the process I prayed two things: 1) that I would be closer to him at the end than I was at the beginning and 2) that I would be honestly able to thank him for the book and for the work represented in it at the end. Normally, the process of work and stress led me away from God as I sacrificed devotions, prayer, service, or loving others in Jesus' name to complete the research I needed to get done. I also felt proud of the work that I had done, so it was difficult to honestly feel that God had contributed to it. After all, I had collected the data, conducted the analysis, and written the papers or chapters. I could thank God with my mouth but in my heart I did not know what I was thanking him for and part of me liked it that way. Rather than get my worth out of Christ's love for me, I got it out of my productivity and professional reputation. Of course these feelings defied reason and the history of my relationship with Christ and all that he had done and provided. I am just being honest.

In any case, I prayed. This began a process of praying and writing and working lasting more than three months. With each new day I would ask God to be a part of what I was doing. For example, if I had a paragraph to write on the connection between FEMA's appointees and disaster preparedness I would ask God to help me craft a good paragraph. Each day, each task I asked God to help, to be a part of what I was doing, to give me words to write, and craft something good in itself.

I think God is woven in to the book I wrote. I am not going to say that the book is a good book or a godly book because I prayed about it. It is a book I could not have written without his help. I do not know how much good there is in the book but what good there is in that book is from him. At the end of the process I can thank him for what was produced because what was produced was not done with my own hands. The process of writing with God this last go-round was like farming. I got behind the mule every day to plow the field but God provided the rain. The quality of the harvest depends on a lot of factors beyond my own tilling, from the size of the field to the quality of the soil and seed. Even a faithful farmer is not always talented. So, there are harvests (books and research) that are bigger and more fruitful and I do not know how mine compares. I do know, however, that this harvest was produced only because God brought rain, enough to yield a harvest at the end. I cannot remember many times feeling closer to God than when I finished that book. I honestly could say, "God, thank you. Even if no one reads this, I am grateful. Put me where you want me and I'll do what you want me to do because you are good and you are trustworthy."

From the choosing of topics to the day-to-day work of reading, thinking, and writing, God can be and wants to be involved in what we do, not just how we do what we do.

4. Conclusion

There are more Christians in my field now than when I began. They study different topics with different methods. We are all different even while similar. We share a common faith and a desire to be faithful; but God's love in us manifests itself quite differently and wonderfully, I think. For all of us, God has not finished with us yet. His work integrating our faith and vocation continues.

Similarly, much of what I have written is as much aspirational, as much hope as practice. God is at work in me, trying to make me the kind of researcher that reflects his glory. We are all a work in progress and all of us engaged in research in this or related fields understand the difficulty of the choices and the pressures we face. These high standards are important and sometimes they seem incredibly high. As one researcher to others, however, these aspirations are also godly.

Staying Faithful: Reflections on an Academic Journey

Howard Louthan
University of Florida
Gainesville, FL
USA

1. Rethinking Models of Success

"Twins?!" The word was like a bolt from heaven. I stared at my wife first in shock, then disbelief and finally simple confusion. It was 1992, a cold and gloomy spring day in Princeton, New Jersey, and something had just gone wrong as we returned from the obstetrician. We had been married for a little less than two years and were coming to the end of our respective PhD programs. Married life had begun with a rush. We spent two months traveling across India and Nepal and then followed it up with an idyllic year of research in Austria as I pursued my work on Renaissance Vienna, and she pushed on with her project on religion in the late Roman Empire. Returning to New Jersey the following year, we discussed the possibility of having children. Though I had intellectually signed on to the idea of starting a family as we taught and finished up our dissertations, the prospect of sleep deprivation, irregular feeding schedules, dirty diapers, tighter finances and perhaps most pointedly limited time for research had remained vague and abstract. Now it came crashing home as I realized that my worst fears had been multiplied by two. This was the first major speed bump I had encountered on what I thought was a fast track to success. I had performed well as an undergraduate. I'd discovered a great love for the study of history and was gratified to find that some of that affection was reciprocated or at least that a number of graduate schools found my application persuasive enough to grant me entry. I had navigated my graduate seminars and exams to the satisfaction of my advisors and had won a couple of competitive outside grants to support my research in Europe. In my estimation, however, my biggest coup was obtaining with my wife a publishing contract for a project we were writing alongside our respective theses. The future looked promising. Little did I realize how the arrival of twin boys in November 1992 would end up transforming my life, my conception of success and my understanding of faithfulness in such profound ways.

From the perspective of hindsight, I see how my own attitudes twenty years ago were very much part of a broader American pattern, a work ethic typical of the middle class. Not much has changed in this respect. Ambitious young children still receive the same message from anxious and over-concerned parents—work hard, overcome obstacles, succeed in your studies and change the world. How many college application essays are filled with these idealistic sentiments—dreams to give Africa clean water, lift India's slum dwellers out of poverty or raise literacy rates in Southeast Asia. Such idealism is not a monopoly of the young. Many would argue that it is implanted in America's genetic code. From the "shining city on the hill" to the "beacon of democracy," so much of this country's history is refracted through this idealistic lens. It has driven foreign policy. It has shaped social and economic priorities, and it has inspired the entertainment industry. It has also influenced the Christian world.

A quick survey of U.S. denominational mission statements reflects the extent to which American Christianity emphasizes the idealistic and transformative potential of the faith. The Presbyterian Church USA emphasizes the importance of "renewing the Church to transform the world." The United States Conference of Catholic Bishops insists that faith must influence the political process. "Our faith demands it. Our teaching calls us to it. Our nation needs it and others depend on it." The Episcopal Church asserts that a "revolution" (of justice and peace) "is precisely what God's work, God's mission is all about." Similar language can be found in the statements of para-church organizations. The rhetoric, in fact, is often martial in nature. Words like "campaign" or "crusade" are frequently bandied about to describe these organizations and their activities as they rally support to change the world in the name of Christ. The Harvey Fellows Program, a program for Christians in graduate school, adopts this same vocabulary in describing its goals. Applicants are sought who will "redeem the structures" of society and become "leaders in strategic occupations." In an interview with D. Michael Lindsay, Dennis Bakke affirmed that the program was established to bring evangelicals into the "ivory tower and the corridors of power." Bakke's interview was part of a broader study compiled by Lindsay examining the ways in which evangelicals have reached positions of power and influence in the world of politics, business, academics, the arts and entertainment. With chapters entitled "Knowledge to Change the World," "A Cultural Revolution," "Executive Influence," and "Move-the-Dial Christianity," Lindsey's book, which features a number of Harvey scholars, captures this culture well. This is an active and ambitious Christianity that seeks to transform its world.

None of this should be surprising. Christian culture reflects for both good and bad the characteristics of its social environment. At the same time there is no doubt that our faith is profoundly revolutionary. Christ came and challenged the values of his society. He gave his followers an alternative code of conduct, one that subverts this world's system and critiques its priorities. We are called to be light and salt, to stand out and make a difference in the world around us. I vividly remember thinking about these issues as I attended a summer institute for Harvey Fellows in the early 90s. Frankly, I felt viscerally torn the entire weekend. Here I was surrounded by an extraordinary group of individuals. I met gifted men and women who were on the fast track for successful careers in business, the law, medicine, politics, the arts and academics. Nearly all of us came from backgrounds where we were pushed to develop our gifts and strive to be the very best. We shared common Christian convictions and recognized the fallen nature of both society at large and our specific professions. We sat through a series of talks intended to inspire us and push us even further. But even as I wanted to soar, I keenly felt the gravitational pull of reality and a bit of guilt as well. I was not home changing diapers or taking my shift calming a crying infant at night. I was not spelling my wife for the time she needed to prepare to teach or revise a chapter of her thesis. It was slowly dawning on me that the twins were not merely a speed bump that would merely slow the dissertation for six months or a year. My new family life was posing an entirely different set of questions that were coming to the fore that Harvey weekend. On the one hand, I was hearing the message—excel and transform your world. On the other, I was feeling the coming need to compromise. Might we as an academic couple who were committed to a family together actually need to lower our professional sights? Might we need to discipline our natural instincts and pursue a more modest scholarly agenda for the sake of each other? These were not the issues or questions I was hearing during the Harvey retreat.

Two decades later, with twins who have now completed their first year of college, this tension remains. I have been blessed, however, to work in an academic field where I have encountered the thought of other Christians who have wrestled with similar questions in different cultural and historical contexts. I have found the work of the Dutch humanist, Desiderius Erasmus (1466-1536), particularly helpful in this regard. Erasmus is commonly regarded as the most important humanist scholar active north of the Alps during the Renaissance period. He was a prolific writer who wrote on topics ranging from child rearing to contemporary politics. He interacted closely with leading Protestant and Catholic reformers without fully committing himself to either side. He was a controversial and complex individual. He was smart, and he knew it. Trying to carve a scholarly niche for himself in a competitive marketplace that makes the contemporary academic scene look tame in comparison, he struggled with his ego. At the same time, he was committed to the ideals of Christ that ran against the predominant values of his culture. He was a keen social critic who observed how his nominally Christian society had slipped its moorings and was now spiritually adrift. Against this backdrop he called for believers to turn back to Scripture and rediscover the essence of Christianity. One of his most eloquent essays, that both exposes the moral bankruptcy of his own society and highlights the radical alternative offered by Christ, can be found in what was arguably the original best-seller of Renaissance Europe, the *Adages*. These were classical proverbs glossed by Erasmus. He provided a brief commentary on the original saying and then launched into a lengthier discourse on its relevance to his culture. They were immensely popular and became one of the most effective vehicles of communicating humanist ideas across Europe. His most powerful statement on Christianity may well have been his exposition on the "Sileni of Alcibiades." The Sileni were small nesting statuettes, a classical equivalent of the popular Russian matryoshka dolls. The outer statue was a grotesque and ugly figure but when opened, one found the hidden image of a god inside. Erasmus considered this an apt metaphor for Christ, "the most extraordinary Silenus all." On the outside "what could be lower or more contemptible measured by popular standards? Obscure and poverty-stricken parents, a humble home; poor himself, he has a few poor men for disciples." On the inside, however, one discovered the true riches of the faith, "the pearl of great price." Erasmus continued by contrasting Christ with the powerful figures of his society in both church and state. Here attractive exteriors, adorned with symbols of power and prestige, were matched with interiors so ugly and repulsive that one was forced to turn away in disgust.

What I have found so compelling in Erasmus is his understanding of this paradox that lies at the heart of the Christian faith. Reflecting on Christ's ministry, he emphasizes the stark and seemingly contradictory contrasts of his life, "in such humility, what grandeur! In such poverty, what riches! In such weakness what immeasurable strength, in such shame, what glory! In such labours, what utter peace!" Erasmus would have been the first to point out that Jesus would not have had a chance in a fellowship competition such as the Harvey Fellows program. He'd be unlikely to survive even the first cut. He did not attend an elite institution. He had taken up a profession that was decidedly not strategic. He was not concerned with entering his society's halls of power but instead spent his active career with a group of undistinguished rustics who were often too dull to understand his teachings. At the same time Erasmus clearly indicates the great problems of power and success--its potential to hollow out our values and convictions, to leave us as shells and husks emptied of virtue and character. As a graduate student and then as a young professor, this message articulated by Erasmus gained greater relevance and meaning the further I progressed in the profession.

My Christian friends and I would comment on the great irony that the real leaders in our specific fields, the individuals often held up as role models or mentors, were in fact often the most morally and personally problematic. One of my favorite stories was about my colleague who completed his PhD at the University of Chicago. One semester he was working with an eminent professor who was clearly a rising star at the school. This specific afternoon the professor had "child-care" responsibilities. He took my friend out with him and his children to the famous Midway, that long green park on the south side of campus. Book in one hand and a soccer ball in the other, he explained that he had found an ideal way to work while watching the kids. He would kick the ball as far as he possibly could and like dogs running after a stick, dispatch his children to retrieve it while he buried himself in the book.

Several years ago, I was fortunate enough to spend two terms at the Institute of Advanced Study in Princeton, New Jersey, a place best known as the academic home of Albert Einstein. The Institute is subdivided into a number of divisions, and I was there as a member of the School of Historical Studies. We were given significant freedom to pursue our respective projects but usually convened as a group for lunch with our "supervisor" who was a permanent professor at the Institute. One of those midday conversations left an especially deep impression on me. A colleague visiting from Britain raised the issue of living a balanced life. Looking us straight in the face, our mentor, a prolific and hard-working scholar, informed us that the whole idea of balance was over-rated. The truly successful person is the one who forgets all notions of proportion completely. Though this advice runs counter to what most of us have heard growing up, he of course was correct in the strictest sense. Those individuals who focus almost exclusively on their narrow area of expertise are the ones most likely to succeed. I just recently survived the college application process for my twin sons. When visiting schools, we routinely heard the rhetoric that their admissions staff was looking for well-rounded applicants. But after experiencing the process from the inside, all of us reached the conclusion that the reality was quite the opposite. Applicants were actually much better off if they had a particular area of excellence that distinguished them and helped them stand out from the crowd.

Is there a need then as Christians to rethink some of the pre-suppositions that may be informing our professional lives? All of us live and work in an incredibly competitive marketplace, and the individuals who do best are often the ones whose behavior is most extreme, whose personal lives wither and whose families (if there are any) bear the brunt of long hours in the office. Let's push this argument to its logical conclusion. Christians are not competing on a level playing field. The ways many of our colleagues make it to the top are options that are not open to us. The ideals manifest in the life of Christ and upheld as a pattern for his followers—service, sacrifice, self-denial—are clearly not the skill set needed to rise to the top in a ruthlessly competitive world. I realize that I am making the extreme case, and most of us are not confronted with such dire or starkly opposing moral choices.

But, still, are we buying into a system that at its essence is antithetical to Christian values and may slowly corrupt us from the inside?

2. The Christian as Dissident

One of the most out-spoken critics of this model is the Christian sociologist, James Davison Hunter. Hunter's most recent book, To *Change the World,* is well worth reading. In it he raises two points in particular that are especially relevant for our discussion. First, he rightly observes that social change is complicated, and too many Christians have been naïve in their assumptions of how their actions can transform the world around them. As an example, he points to William Wilberforce, one of the great heroes of the evangelical world. Wilberforce is often popularly construed as the conscience of England, the man who almost single-handedly shamed his country into ending the slave trade. But as Hunter reminds us and as any good historian would affirm, the abolition of slavery in the British Empire was extraordinarily complicated. This is not to diminish the conviction and courage of Wilberforce but to place him in a broader context. His individual contribution was a small part of a broader phenomenon that culminated with abolition. Indeed, many of the factors that contributed to this outcome were far from altruistic but based on national self-interest and reflected strikingly paternalistic attitudes. Hunter contends that many Christian groups who want to "change the world" today base their efforts on the dubious assumption that history can be "controlled and managed." The second issue is one already alluded to, the problem of power. Power is a dangerous dynamic, and those who seek to grasp it to change the world for good are often transformed themselves in the process. Tragically, Christians both individually and as a group can end up developing those negative characteristics they had so idealistically set out to reform. Their strategic vision can become a "capitulation to the worst elements of the contemporary culture it claims to be redeeming."

Whether or not one entirely agrees with Hunter's arguments, the warnings he raises should be taken seriously by all of us. Over the past two decades as I have thought through my own calling in academics and these difficult issues of power and social change, I have found a very different model through my own work in central Europe. In 1989 as a graduate student, I spent a portion of my summer in Prague studying the Czech language. As social and political tensions were rising across the Eastern Bloc, this was a fascinating time to be in Czechoslovakia. In fact I had the opportunity to participate in my first riot that August when the city's inhabitants commemorated the 1968 Soviet invasion by turning out en masse in Prague's central square. Drawn to the allure of that spectacle, I watched enrapt as riot police descended and sought to clear out and cordon off the area. The crowds pushed back and began to taunt them with chants. It started slowly and indistinctly at first but over time even with my rudimentary Czech, I was able to understand their cry. They were calling for the man who, though still imprisoned, had become the symbol of their dissent. As the riot shields and batons came out, and we were forcibly pushed down the city's side streets, the chants for Václav Havel grew ever louder and insistent. Though I left before the water cannons started firing, I was hooked. Even though our teachers, state employees all, were obviously hesitant to say much about Havel, he was the topic of conversation among us students. I had to find out more about this charismatic playwright and dissident.

The first place I turned was an essay he wrote in 1978 entitled, "The Power of the Powerless," an analysis of the role and function of dissent in totalitarian societies. I found the article uncannily insightful on my own identity as a Christian and calling as a young professional. Havel tells the story of an anonymous greengrocer living in a socialist state. A local party official has given him a placard with the slogan, "Workers of the World Unite." Without much thought or conviction, he dutifully places the sign between his onions and carrots. What, queries Havel, is the significance of this act? It is unlikely that the grocer has any strong feelings about the ironworkers of China or other members of the global proletariat. He simply puts up the sign to avoid any trouble, to show his superiors that he is loyal and obedient. In doing so, however, he is adding one small voice of assent to a larger system that is built on lies. Even though he couldn't care less about Bolivian miners, by placing the poster among his vegetables he is agreeing to the rules of the system and as Havel says is "living within a lie." What would happen, though, if one day something snapped, and the greengrocer decided to stop playing the game? He stopped putting up signs, ceased voting in farcical elections and started expressing his opinions at political meetings. He begins "living within the truth." The small everyday actions of a powerless grocer have exposed the system for what it is. As Havel observes:

He has shattered the world of appearances, the fundamental pillar of the system. He has upset the power structure by tearing apart what holds it together…He has shown everyone that it is possible to live within the truth.

Over the years I have reread this essay a number of times and continue to find it helpful. The Christian is in many respects a dissident, and how we live in this alien system where the rules are derived from lies and bolstered by illusions is at the very heart of our calling. God's primary call for our lives is not success but faithfulness. I am sure that all of us can point to tragic examples of well-intentioned Christians who climbed their professional ladders only to discover that it was they who had changed, not the system, by the time they reached the top. Our greatest witness is how we live in a world and workplace deeply corrupted by sin. Like Havel's grocer, we can through faithful lives expose the system for what is. If success and the chance to influence our profession for good come along the journey, then we can be thankful for the opportunities that God has given us. But to use Aristotelian terminology, our professional successes or failures are accidents or characteristics of our work. They are not its essence. Faithfulness comes first. All else follows.

3. Three Practical Lessons

I would like to close by moving from the abstract to the specific and, hopefully, practical. As an academic couple with twins (and shortly thereafter a third child, all before tenure-track jobs), how have we negotiated these challenges while seeking to remain faithful to God's call? I will highlight three general sets of lessons that we are continuing to learn over these two decades of marriage and work.

Downward Mobility

After a year of temporary contracts for both my wife and myself, I was fortunate enough to be hired in a tenure-track position at a top-20 research university. It was a great job working with smart colleagues and fabulous students at an institution that was ambitious and willing to spend money to improve its standing and reputation. It was the type of place where I could pitch an idea to a dean and leave his office that day with $25,000 to run a conference. My wife had given up an opportunity at another school to come with me. We had vague hopes that some type of position might open up for her down the line. Over time it became clear, however, that a permanent job was unlikely to materialize. Though I eventually earned tenure, we were still very concerned with her situation. Both of us remained active on the job market, and in the end we received an offer for two positions at a large state university. Though the move was a no-brainer, I still felt pangs of regret. I was giving up a higher-profile position and the resources of a wealthy private institution. I was trading down in prestige and in all likelihood moving to a school where I would have less of a chance attracting highly-motivated graduate students.

In hindsight, it is clear that the sacrifices I have made, though real, have been relatively small, and what we have gained as a couple and family has more than compensated for what I as an individual may have lost. Yes, I did give up a good job, but I was fortunate enough to move to another position that, especially in today's market, is highly attractive. Still, the larger point remains. Unfortunately, the evangelical world has not been in the vanguard in terms of gender equality and sensitivity to the challenges of dual-career couples. Here many of us can make a difference by our willingness to sacrifice personal ambition for a broader good. Our lives and the decisions that we make, even when they may take us from the center of our professional world to the periphery, illustrate our allegiance to a higher calling. Not all of us, of course, are married or have children, but still the issue of "downward mobility" is relevant for all including those who are single. Might God be calling us to live and work in a healthier culture than the highly competitive hot-house environment that is typical of positions at the top of our respective professions? There is obviously no single answer to this difficult question. God places us in different situations, but at the very least we need to consider the demands of our job and its potential impact on our broader lives.

Living Locally

My wife and I were very active in our local InterVarsity chapters during both our undergraduate and graduate careers.

My wife, in fact, served as an IV staff worker in the U.S. and abroad before returning to graduate school and an academic career. InterVarsity nourished us spiritually and gave us an opportunity for ministry. Both of us naively thought that once we became faculty we would be inundated with invitations to speak at conferences and engage closely with staff workers and students from a variety of Christian para-church ministries. Though a few opportunities have arisen, we have more often felt neglected or ignored by some of these groups. In time we realized how silly it was to feel snubbed. Many of these groups are struggling organizationally while their leaders may be intimidated by Christian faculty.

So instead of waiting for that timid knock on the door, we took the initiative. God was calling us to be attentive to our local setting, to be faithful in the environment where he placed us. One of the needs we saw was with Christian graduate students. We applied for a three-year grant that funded a dinner and discussion group to consider the unique personal, professional and spiritual challenges of graduate students who feel called to academia. We invited other Christian faculty to share their insights and experience, while also bringing in local pastors who have very little experience with academic life and frequently do not understand the special needs and pressures that these graduate students are facing.

We also began collaborating with a local Christian Study Center. The director, a PhD himself from the University of Virginia, was interested in genuine dialogue with the university community (not always true with these type of centers!). From early Christianity to the Reformation, we have run a number of speaker series with the center that have successfully brought together both secular and Christian faculty. My wife, in fact, has edited with a colleague in Jewish Studies a volume with Cornell University Press entitled, *Faithful Narratives: Historians, Religion, and the Challenge of Objectivity* a project that grew out of a three-semester series sponsored by the Study Center and numerous departments and centers on campus. The larger point in both these examples is that we merely responded to local needs and opportunities. Indeed, one of the biggest opportunities we have is the simple gift of hospitality and friendship. Regularly entertaining graduate and undergraduate students at our home is not very difficult, but at least at our institution it is surprising how infrequently it is actually done.

The Messiness of Life

Rereading what I have already written, I am afraid that I may be creating a false impression that my activities have been carefully thought through and strategically planned. Honestly the past two decades of marriage, family and professional life have been a blur of movement too often occurring at breakneck speed. Though I have attempted to control the pace of life, to balance out my various responsibilities, more often than not I feel that it is all getting beyond me. Family life is one example. I look back to the time I started graduate school without a wife, without children, without many responsibilities and marvel how quickly it all changed and how fast the chaos descended (and has never lifted). There was one period of six years in which my children ended up attending a different school every fall. I still have a file of emails from my wife sharing with me the daily struggles of managing three energetic boys when I went off solo to Prague for several months on a fellowship. Professionally, too, I have not always been able to regulate the workload. Though I have tried to act prudently, to reflect carefully before taking on a project, I do not always succeed and frequently end up over-committed. Spiritually as well, I have faced parallel challenges. I entered graduate school with tidy theological categories that, though helpful for a time, could not in the end encompass and explain the complexities of life. Without jettisoning Christian essentials, I have come to appreciate the messiness of faith where not all issues are resolved, and ambiguity often remains.

More often than not, I feel hopelessly compromised as a scholar and teacher, as a father, husband and son. How do I stay faithful with all these demands? Too often I have responded in one of two ways. When tired or exhausted at the end of a busy day or a particularly difficult stretch of work, I have given in to feelings of hopelessness and guilt, of knowing that I can never measure up to impossibly high standards. On the other hand, when I am fresher and more energetic, I deceive myself into thinking that I can somehow manage it all. Of course, neither response is appropriate or accurately reflects our true situation. I am slowly coming to realize that when God calls us to be faithful, he is also calling us to embrace the messiness of life. Indeed, God wants us to be in a position of spiritual dependency, to acknowledge our inadequacies, limitations and failures. To feel off-balance is not a bad thing, for it forces all of us to turn daily if not hourly to the one source of adequacy there is in life.

Failing Faithfully: Christian Reflections on Ambition, Influence and Success

Justin Denholm
Centre for Applied Christian Ethics
Ridley Melbourne Mission and Ministry College
Australia

1. Introduction

"You are a person with many gifts and a calling for your life. You have the opportunity to succeed in your chosen field and to glorify God with your influence. Your competence and intelligence will attract people to faith in Christ. If you were to turn away from using your skills and abilities to further your career, you would not be a faithful steward of what you have been given."

I don't know how you felt as you read these words. I'm convinced, though, that what you've just read is perhaps the most dangerous paragraph I've ever written. Every word in it has been said to me and many others; maybe you've heard these things as well. The more I reflect on them, though, the more convinced I am that they are dangerous words with potentially disastrous consequences--the more so because they contain some element of truth.

This chapter is intended as a theological reflection on success and ambition from a Christian perspective. I write as a doctor, academic and ethicist who finds these aspects of work difficult and struggles with their application. In my life, I've been encouraged and provided with opportunities for leadership both in the church and the workplace and find myself uncertain about how to engage with them faithfully; perhaps these words reflect only my own temptations and longing for influence and validation. It is my hope and prayer as I write, though, that these ideas might challenge you as you think about your future, just as they have, and continue, to challenge and change me.

2. Created, Fallen and Waiting

It is instructive to begin with a theological overview of work and our relationship to it. Christian theology of work often starts from a basis in our nature as people created in the image of God. While interpreted in different ways, this commonly reminds us that we are made to be like our God, who is creative and relational, and who takes pleasure in the world he has made. Productive activity for humans was present from the very beginning of creation, with God intending for his people to be active and engaged in meaningful oversight and care for the world (Genesis 1:28). Our work today echoes this calling, as we continue to have responsibility for our world, and find it natural to long to engage with it in creative and productive ways.

Our understanding of our relationship with work does not, however, begin and end with creation. At the Fall, the relationship between humanity, God and the world was broken (Genesis 3). While the Fall clearly fractures every element of this world and our experience of it, work is singled out as an activity which will become burdensome and painful (Gen 3:17-19). The impact of the Fall is not merely that the previously productive activities we were to be involved in are now difficult to accomplish, or that the good goals for which our work aims are now elusive. Clearly these things are true, but to limit the effect of the Fall to these frustrations is to neglect the impact that it has on us as fallen human beings. Taking our fallenness seriously also has to mean that our ability to appreciate and rightly perceive the proper goals and aims of our work is also compromised; alone, we do not even know what we do not know.

Finally, our world was created and has fallen, but now waits to be redeemed (Rev 21:1-4). Christians are people with a hope for a new Earth, one which will be restored fully to right relationships between itself, God and humanity. This is a process that has been begun through the death and resurrection of Jesus Christ, but waits to be completed with his return. We long for that time and wait in anticipation, knowing that the work of remaking this world is not ours but Christ's (Romans 8:18-25).

So what are the implications of this theology for our understanding of work now? Well, we are all created and fallen, and it is appropriate that we feel the tension between these poles in our work as we wait for Christ's return. Our fallen condition does not mean that we will never take pleasure in our work, that we will never see it have a positive impact on the world around us, that we will never please God in our capacity as workers. These things are good gifts from God's creation, and are part of our hope as we long for the world to come. It does mean, though, that our desires and aims are unreliable guides to how God would have us work, and that our satisfaction can never be its yardstick. It has been said, and frequently repeated, that our vocation is found when our 'great joy intersects with the world's great need'. My conviction, though, is that a properly biblical understanding of work should lead us to be suspicious of both the reliability of our emotions as guide and our ability to evaluate the true needs of the world around us. We are people who long for the time when our world will be restored, when we will be in harmony with God and the new creation; but that time is not yet fully come. For now, we continue to work and strive, but we also must be people who wait. We wait, secure that the hope we have will not be disappointed, and our struggles now will one day glorify God in ways we cannot imagine.

These broad theological themes provide a backdrop against which to consider the statements with which this chapter opened. While there are many ideas permeating these statements, I will focus on three, related to our understanding of vocations, stewardship and success.

3. Vocation: Whose Calling?

Our concept of vocation often begins from questions like "What do you want me to do, God?" or "Who should I be?"

These are powerful questions, and Christians ask them in a genuine desire for God's heart and a longing to be certain of their place within God's ordering of the world. Many Christians have done great things after finding an answer--things we remember and appreciate and which act to strengthen our own faith even generations and centuries later.

The concept that we might seek our vocation has historically derived much from the call to ordained ministry, to the priesthood. If entering the ministry means being set apart, for instance from marriage in some traditions, it could seem clear that one was either called vocationally or was not. The later development and extension of our understanding of vocation meant that Christians have felt increasingly free to understand their work in this way, even in so-called 'secular' fields. My own field of medicine, of course, features heavily in this regard. While it has been relatively unusual to hear Christian airline pilots or fast food workers describe their paid work as vocational, the language and notion are relatively ubiquitous amongst Christian doctors, and, I notice, increasingly so amongst other Christian professionals and academics. Those of us who share faith within the academy often understand our work as, in some way, fulfilling a task God has for us in this world. What I'd like to suggest, though, is that our work is not 'vocational' in that it does not define the boundaries of how we are to serve God. While our work provides opportunities to serve faithfully, labeling it as vocational runs the risk that we can view our service at work as somehow more important than our service in other ways.

An example might help. On Sunday morning, you will find me in church. However, there is a fair chance that you won't see me in the service, because I have spent many mornings downstairs in our crèche (nursery). Typically, this consists of an hour or so of reading children's stories, doling out pasta and fruit and separating screaming toddlers. It's probably not your idea of a good time, and frankly, it's not high on my list either. I would much rather sit upstairs, listen to the sermon and enjoy a few moments of peace. In spite of this, when I consider my ministry areas and the different ways in which I am involved, crèche is consistently what I feel most passionate about. It is the aspect of my ministry that I recognize most clearly as being 'vocational', more than being a doctor or a researcher. Why? Well, one reason is that it supports evangelism. Taking care of the children in this way liberates people to hear and reflect on the gospel. It frees visitors to concentrate on the message, and it frees long-time Christians to worship together, to have good conversations and make new connections. It also encourages parents to come back to church. Perhaps just as importantly, though, I don't necessarily love it. I don't get any glory or reward or personal advancement from doing it, and I think that helps my service to the church in this way in being relatively non-conflicted and unconstrained.

By contrast, my sense of being able to serve God through my medical work has been much more variable and conflicted. At times in my career, I have felt very much that medicine was just a workplace like any other. I worked to earn money and support my family, and I was grateful that medicine could provide that opportunity. I recognized that the hospitals I worked in were good places to meet others, to have evangelistic conversations with other staff and patients, and I valued the workplace for these opportunities. It seemed to me, though, that these were opportunities that could come up in any workplace – nothing special about medicine here. I remember talking with my hairdresser about evangelism at work and thinking that there were far more similarities than differences between our workplaces.

None of this is to deny that we have wonderful opportunities to serve God through our workplaces. Certainly, my experience has been that medical practice allows participation in the lives of others at some of the most difficult moments in life, and offers moments that God can use powerfully. For me, there was one day that brought this home most strongly. Two patients under my team were in hospital, and both were clearly close to death. The first had been in for a few weeks with a metastatic cancer, while the second came in suddenly, with abdominal pain that quickly declared itself as a bleeding aortic aneurysm. While we sat waiting for the surgical team to take her away, the urgency of the situation pushed me to ask, nervously, if I could pray for her. To my relief, she answered eagerly, and as we prayed together she cried out to the Jesus she had forgotten about since her childhood. Afterwards, she was swept away to surgery where a long operation was cut short by her on-table arrest and death. As far as I can know anything in this life, I think her last waking moments were spent asking Jesus to remember her, and it was my privilege as a doctor to be there with her.

This stands in stark contrast to perhaps an hour later, as I sat with my first patient upstairs on the ward. I took the momentum of the morning into a conversation with her about death, and about what might come afterwards. As eagerly as my prayer was accepted in the morning, it was thrown back at me in the afternoon, as she laughed at me and said she looked forward to being in hell with her friends. I fumbled out of the room, thinking that I might try again another day. Of course, it turned out that I didn't have another day, as she died later that afternoon.

Now that is a day that stays with you for life. I am grateful that God used my position as a doctor to put me in those situations. I hope that I represented Christ faithfully, and I know I will one day be held to account for what happened. After reflecting about this for a number of years, though, I don't believe that my position and opportunities as a doctor are fundamentally different from those I have as an ethicist, a father, a husband or a crèche worker. In each I have opportunities to live faithfully, chances to connect with other people and moments into which I can sometimes shine the gospel, or fail to. My vocation in its entirety includes the full range of things that God is calling me to – it is a comprehensive call on my life in every detail, not a job that I come home from to unwind.

4. Stewardship: Whose Gifts?

A friend told me recently that she felt compelled to rush back to work after her daughter was born. She explained that her years of study and training meant that not to do so would be to waste what God had given her and that it would be bad stewardship to be at home with her child. Last week, in a conversation after church, another told me that he wondered sometimes whether he should work in a volunteer context, but couldn't because God had provided him with a high paying, influential job. He had the capacity to give away money to support God's work, he reasoned, and so it would be bad stewardship to walk away from it to take up volunteer work.

It's not my intention to suggest that my friends' workplaces are unimportant, or that their ability to serve God faithfully in those contexts is not real. Both of them, however, used the language of 'stewardship' to justify continuing in their paid employment. In my experience, this is common amongst Western Christians, and I think worth exploring further. What are we stewarding, and what does it mean to do it well?

A steward looks after something for another person. One important aspect of stewardship is about the creation mandate in Genesis 1:28. Humanity here is tasked with caring for the Earth and 'every living thing'. In the New Testament, the paradigmatic passage about stewardship is the story Jesus tells – the parable of the talents (Mt 25:14-30). The owner gives various servants different amounts of money to safeguard in his absence. Then, when he returns, he questions them about how they have used what he has given them. Those who have used their talents productively have made him a profit, but the servant who simply returns the talent is rejected and evicted by the owner.

I have often heard this latter passage read as if it refers to our skills or our 'talents'. Of course, in this story, the 'talent' is a measure of precious metal, probably gold, rather than the ability of the servants. Jesus, though, is telling this story as part of a series of lessons about the Kingdom of God. He is doing so in Jerusalem several days before he will be crucified, and the message of the parable is about much more than our personal skills. This is about the gospel, about the precious gift that the church has been entrusted with until the Kingdom of God is fully realized. The servant thought that he could preserve what he had been given by keeping it intact, safe and secret. Jesus, though, wants the gospel message to go out and the Kingdom of God to grow.

In our strongly individualistic cultures, it is critical that we notice that stewardship is not about how you as an individual care for what you have been given. In both the Genesis and Matthew passages above, the imperative is for us collectively; the creation mandate to care for the Earth is for all people, and the message of the parable of the talents is for the Church. Our individual skills and abilities are not primarily what we are stewarding; as Christians, we are collectively stewards of creation and the gospel. Our guiding questions as individuals, then, should be about contributing to the Church. How can we use our skills and abilities to help the Church be a good steward? How can we serve the Church? How can we ensure that we are both caring for the environment and advancing the gospel? These are questions that will be of more use to us in faithfully using our skills, then trying to determine what use will fulfil us more perfectly or optimize our individual effectiveness.

If we are serious about stewarding the skills and opportunities God has given us, we need to use them in the ways he puts before us rather than in the ways we might choose. Maybe your gift for languages and interpersonal skills means that you should be a diplomat, or maybe it means that you can connect your church with the refugee community in your hometown, or the local primary school. Maybe using your qualifications as an engineer for a career in mining is a good idea, or maybe you would serve the gospel better by walking away and investing your time in family and the local community. God is not dependent on our career track; he can be glorified by our skills and history in so many ways we can't even imagine. The things that are great in the Kingdom of God will surprise us.

5. Leadership, Ambition and Success: Whose Glory?

It is extremely tempting to approach our fields with a desire to reform them for God. This is particularly the case for those of us who inhabit workplaces and locations that are heavily secular in nature. Many of us long for increasing power and influence in these fields, with which we intend to shape them in ways that glorify God and attract people to him. We need to understand, though, that our ability to accomplish these goals is limited, and our motivation to do so is mixed.

We commonly look to examples like Daniel and Joseph as faithful people of God who succeed in the world. Clearly, there are times when God's purposes coincide with worldly success and influence. God can certainly use us as the CEO of a major corporation or as Nobel-winning scientists. Such people have served him faithfully before, and he can surely use them again. The problem I have, though, is that it doesn't seem at all clear to me that God intends for us to seek to serve him in these ways. Think of Daniel, kidnapped and pressganged into service, or Joseph, sold into slavery. These men rose to power obliquely; they sought to follow God faithfully regardless of circumstance, and were used in ways that seem 'successful' to us. For every Daniel or Joseph, though, is a Jeremiah or Hosea; people who follow God's call in ways that lead them to suffer ridicule and be sidelined.

God's call may not lead to the corner office that I think would suit my talents perfectly, but to caring for my disabled neighbor. Perhaps even more difficult is the idea that I may be asked to continue to serve God in my field of work but be "mediocre" in order to devote myself to the work of the local church or some other end.

In some situations, faithfulness may be rewarded in worldly pursuits. Traits like honesty may be recognized and lead to advancement in some fields. It seems to me far from inevitable that this will be the case, however. It is at least as likely that following Christ will lead us to worldly failure. Our priorities for serving our families and our churches may mean that we are less committed to our workplaces than others, and in some fields honesty may not be a pathway to career development! More fundamentally, though, we follow a crucified God and walk the road to Calvary. We serve a God who is most glorified in us when we are weak and powerless. We are people who are told we should be pitied if we do not have resurrection and vindication to look forward to. The question I ask myself, then, is 'how likely is it that faithful abandonment to his service will lead to a life of worldly influence and respect'?

So what does this mean for me as a Christian who aspires to lead? Well, most bluntly, it leads me to distrust my reasons for wanting to lead and influence. As much as I tell myself that my motivation is to serve God, to influence others in ways that glorify him, to lead my field toward aims that please him, I don't believe me. While Christian faith should not mean that we can never lead or be successful in worldly terms, I am increasingly convinced that these things should be thrust upon us reluctantly rather than be things we strive for.

6. Conclusions

Is it possible to conclude a work in progress? These issues continue to be at the forefront of my thinking, and I don't believe that God has finished shaping me yet. I think that God has been teaching me some tough lessons about myself and my arrogant grasping for status--some rough edges that have been battered by sustained theological reflection on these issues. I don't know whether this process is part of God preparing me to go a different way from the academic career I had envisaged, but whatever the case, I want to be sure that my heart is to serve him wherever this life is heading.

From where I sit right now, my reflections on vocation, stewardship and ambition have led me to one central insight that has disrupted and affected me most: in this life, the power of the resurrection is the strength to be powerless. Ours is not a faith that leads to glory in this world but rejection. What we believe should make us different from the world around us rather than popular. 'Shining like stars' will get you noticed but not necessarily applauded! Following Christ faithfully in this world can be a difficult path to walk; it is the road to the cross.

Instead of looking to succeed for Christ, perhaps it is possible to grasp hold of a vision for failing faithfully. By this I don't mean working badly or not trying, but serving God fearlessly wherever he takes us and being prepared to fall short in the eyes of the world. Are we prepared to follow Christ if it means reckless disregard for our own success or influence in favor of service to the gospel?

The image that I want to leave you with is that of the man who found a treasure buried in a field and sold everything he owned to buy it. We often think about the sacrifices this story envisages, but more and more I find myself picturing what his friends and colleagues thought of him. How dumb he must have looked to people around him for abandoning everything he owned! How crazy his choices must have seemed to those who didn't know that the treasure was real! I wonder what my colleagues and friends who are not Christians think about my choices and the way I live my life. Does it make sense to the world around me – does my atheist neighbor wonder why on earth I would make the choices I have? If not, do I really understand what this treasure is worth?

Reflections on Family-Career Balance

Matthew T. Cabeen
Harvard University
USA

1. Introduction: A Dilemma

A colleague of mine—call him Will—is another postdoctoral fellow in my biology lab at Harvard. He is a few years ahead of me, and recently completed his job search. Will landed two assistant-professor positions: one at a university in Texas, the other at a Boston-area university. The offers themselves were quite different. The Texas job would have a higher profile and would come with several hundred thousand more dollars to start his lab, allowing him to buy more equipment and recruit better personnel. The Boston job, while coming with a smaller start-up package and less prestige, had an important personal advantage.

Will's wife, Jill, is an associate professor at another Boston-area university, and she is about one year away from tenure.

Will and Jill have two young daughters aged four and one. The university in Texas tried to find Jill a tenure-track position but came up empty. By taking the job in Texas, Will would have to live apart from his wife and young children for at least a year, at which point she could again try to find a position in Texas once she was tenured. If he takes the job in Boston, the smaller start-up package will limit the research he can do, potentially affecting his entire career.

Our advisor told Will to take the job in Texas. "Consider your whole career," he said. "This is just one year." But is depriving his family of their husband and father for a year a worthy sacrifice for the sake of a more promising career trajectory? Can he count on Jill being able to find a position in Texas next year? Will is torn. What should he do?

The enterprise of finding an appropriate balance between career and family is sufficiently important that many organizations have offices devoted to helping their employees find it (at Harvard, this is called "Work/Life"). Among those populating the world's most prestigious universities and companies, there is often a bias toward favoring career, even to the detriment of family or personal life. I often see this bias among my friends and colleagues, and it takes different forms: the single person with a demanding job but no time for a romantic relationship; the couple delaying pregnancy (or even marriage) until they can reach some career milestone; the couple who live far from one another so that both spouses can pursue their careers; the couple whose marriage is crumbling even as their careers soar. For many of my friends and colleagues, irrespective of their religious and cultural values, there is a feeling of unease or dissatisfaction associated with this career-centric state of affairs. In fact, the difficulty of finding career-family balance has recently been placed in the national spotlight with the publication of an essay titled "Why Women Still Can't Have It All" by a Princeton professor and stateswoman, Anne-Marie Slaughter.

For Christians, balancing the demands of career with family considerations has a special character. We affirm our God-given talents, strive for excellence in all our endeavors, and believe in the dignity and importance of work. At the same time, our most ancient Christian traditions teach us that marriage and family life are vocations to which we are called by God—sacred cornerstones not only of our lives but of a just society. As such, our duties and responsibilities as spouses and parents are bound up in our relationship with God and our status as followers of Jesus Christ. For a married person, serving spouse and children is one of the most important and immanent ways that one renders service to God.

I have written this book chapter as a guide for thinking about and reflecting upon the proper place of work and family in our lives. It's not just for married couples with children; the considerations I will discuss are instructive even when seeking a mate or considering whether or when to start a family. I intend to uncover moral principles that form a reliable and broadly applicable basis for making just decisions about our families and careers. Of course, the application of broad principles in specific cases will produce variations in the exact courses of action we pursue. These variations will depend on the unique set of conditions faced by each one of us at different times in our lives. Fortunately, moral principles provide a firm foundation for decision making. They merit our prayerful and thoughtful consideration as we continue to seek a vibrant family life, a satisfying career, and—most importantly—the face of Christ.

2. My Family and Career

It may be useful to have a brief description of my own career and family life, so that the reader may understand the context within which I have considered the questions at hand. I am a husband, father, and microbiologist. I have been married to my wife, Rose, for six years. We wed during my fifth year of graduate school at Yale University. From the outset of our relationship, we agreed that we both felt a strong calling to family life and that we desired a large family, if it were intended by God. We also agreed that she would forego a career in favor of raising our children and managing our household, despite our having only my graduate-student stipend as income. By God's grace, Rose gave birth to our first son, Thomas, nine months after our wedding. Our second son, Benjamin, was born sixteen months after Tommy and two weeks after I defended my PhD.

We then moved to Boston so I could take a postdoctoral position at Harvard. Priced out of Cambridge, we live a half-hour subway ride away in a two-bedroom apartment in Dorchester, known as one of Boston's "rougher" neighborhoods (it's a lot like New Haven). Our third son, Henry, is two years old as I write, and Tommy and Ben are five and four.

I am thankful that my academic career has so far been successful. My PhD advisor's career soared during my time in her lab, and during my tenure there I authored or co-authored several articles, wrote grants, and presented at international meetings. I was awarded competitive graduate fellowships, including the Harvey Fellowship, a fellowship specifically for Christian graduate students. Now, as a postdoc, I am doing my research in a very well-established lab with a famous mentor and am funded by a prestigious fellowship. It is difficult to predict how things will turn out in the end, but I am on the same path traveled by many who are now successful professors. I desire to be a professor, and feel the attraction of teaching at a top university. At the same time, I am given pause by what I observe among professors whose careers I admire; few of them have enjoyed the kind of vibrant family life that I envision for my own family. Can the family life I desire co-exist with the career I am drawn to? If so, what will it look like? Is God calling me to reject what is widely regarded as career success for the sake of my family? How can I most effectively listen for His will? Can I maintain a robust family life while pursuing an ambitious career track? If so, what will my life look like? I must ask these questions again and again as my family grows and my career develops.

From the time of our engagement, Rose and I have continually communicated about our goals, desires, and expectations. As we succeed or fail in meeting our goals, we re-evaluate and adapt as our situation changes. Let me give just a few examples. We try to make both dinnertime and our boys' bedtime "sacred." I always try to come home in time for dinner, but Rose tries to be flexible and forgiving if I occasionally work late. If I need more time in lab, I go earlier in the morning and she takes care of the boys when they rise. Rose dislikes it when I travel for work without the family (I do love to travel and did so quite often before I had a family). Thus, I now carefully evaluate the importance of meetings and conferences, choose local ones if I can, and try to take my family to the few faraway meetings I attend and extend them into vacations (this has led to some great memories!). Finally, I try to be truly present for Rose and the boys when I am at home. I try not to use the computer or do work during our time in the evening. Again, if I have a pressing deadline or something important to do, I will go into the office early or work after the boys have gone to bed and after I have had time to talk and be present to Rose.

I happen to think that goals like being present to your family members and having a time (like mealtime) consistently set apart for family togetherness have considerable merit. The larger point is that the particular goals for each couple or family should first be honestly and amicably discussed. Then, they should be practiced daily with a Holy Spirit-empowered attitude of mutual love and service (and forgiveness!).

3. What is a Successful Career?

We all claim to want a successful career. Who would want an unsuccessful one? But exactly what constitutes career success can be less clear. Typically, if we say "Jen has a successful career," we mean that Jen makes a lot of money, has acquired prestige or influence, or both. Perhaps she is personally unfulfilled, but that doesn't enter into our definition. If she told us she is unhappy, we then might say that she has a successful career but is unhappy rather than that she has an unsuccessful career. Similarly, if Bob is a physician who serves HIV-positive patients in Rwanda, we would all agree that he is doing important and worthy work that is probably personally fulfilling (and even successful medically!). If we were describing Bob to friends at a cocktail party, we might call him good or self-less—but probably not as having a successful career.

I submit that this definition of a "successful career" that we commonly use in casual conversation actually has its basis in a general assumption that the acquisition of wealth and prestige are the primary goals of a career. I question that assumption. I advocate a simpler definition of career success that more closely follows the everyday definition of the word "success." Think about a successful experiment, a successful journey, a successful training program, a successful diet, or a successful product. In all these cases, success is defined by the outcome of an action having met its objectives; something is unsuccessful insofar as it fails to meet some or all of its objectives. As with any other undertaking, a career is successful if it meets the objectives that we assign to it.

Therefore, in our consideration of balancing career and family life, we must ask: what are the objectives of my career? What are the objectives of my family life? When I say "balancing career and family life," I am speaking of two sets of objectives (career and family life) that may at times be in competition or conflict (hence the need to balance). Therefore, we need to know, with clarity, the identity of the objectives that for us constitute "career."

Earning abundant money and achieving prestige or influence are not unjust per se. We need money as an instrumental good directed toward providing the things that we and our dependents need. Money is also a vehicle of generosity toward others, especially the poor and downtrodden persons so beloved by Jesus. Prestige and influence are powerful assets that can be used to promote the causes of justice and truth. At the same time, it is dangerous to make wealth and power our goals. We must continually re-evaluate: how much money is enough for me and my family so that we can meet our family life goals? What things am I willing or unwilling to do in order to increase my income? What level of prestige or influence do I seek? What paths do I plan to take in order to get there? In many professional fields, influence and prestige are gained through a combination of hard work and favorable circumstance. Can I still be satisfied if unfavorable circumstances prevent me from fully achieving my goals? Might circumstances (favorable or no) represent the hand of God guiding my journey? What are the responsibilities that go with different levels of influence? Will they take me away from my family, or might they conflict with my goals regarding family life? What family goals am I unwilling to compromise?

Fortunately, we can eschew the common definition of career success for ourselves. There is nothing forcing us to accept money and prestige as primary or even important goals; in fact, their pursuit can be a stumbling block that retards spiritual growth. Jesus' own life, and the lives of the saints who best imitate Him, bear witness to a different set of priorities. In God's economy, whoever wants to be first must be the servant of all. We are commanded not to chase after material things, for our Father knows what we need. This frees us to seek first the kingdom of God and righteousness, and He will give us what we need. Notably, a shift in our goals and priorities does not mean that we should no longer work hard or pursue excellence, as if seeking God's kingdom means ignoring practical affairs. What it does mean is that we use different criteria to evaluate how things are going and to make decisions at junctures. Consider these alternative questions regarding our careers: is my job helping others? Am I able to bear witness to Christ through my work and collegial interactions? Does my career allow me to achieve more or fewer of my goals for family life? Does it encourage or discourage my spiritual development? Does it bring out virtues or vices in me? Do I like who I am when I'm at work? Am I a positive influence in my work, community and in my social communities? Does my job place undue stress on me, my spouse, or my children? Do I feel like I have the time and energy to listen to the Lord in prayer, follow his leading, and serve him in concrete ways?

Two more things are worth remembering. First, wealth, prestige, and many other measures of career success are under God's control, and are subordinate to our obedience in matters of faith and morals. "It is God who judges: He brings one down, he exalts another." Some persons may be called by God to great influence, like Daniel or Joseph. We often cite these men as examples of persons placed by God in positions of secular power. This is rightly so, but Daniel and Joseph are notable for reasons other than the secular power they happened to have. Let us be mindful that these men steadfastly followed God in the face of temptation. Would I face the lions' den, tell the king bad news, or refuse wealth and honor the way Daniel did? Would I have the courage never to compromise my faith, even if faced with loss of everything? Would I follow God as Joseph did, even when it looked as if his life were going nowhere, sold into slavery by his own brothers or thrown into prison in a foreign land? Can I emulate these men by letting God place me, improbably, in positions of power? Or am I committed to seeing to it myself? We must acknowledge that others, like the rich young man (Mt 19) or the Apostle Paul, are called from wealth, power, or prestige to humility. Even today, God calls men and women every day to renounce the world and commit themselves to the humility of ministry or religious life. Can I freely and joyfully accept either call from the Lord?

Second, "what is good for my career" can often simply mean "what I want for me." I repeatedly must remind myself that, as a married man, my 'I' now expands to include the good of my wife and family. To be consistent with love and justice, my career objectives must include the whole well-being of my family (beyond just meeting their financial needs). I must leave behind the more self-centered and self-directed ways of life that were appropriate when I was a single man.

4. Two Spouses, Two Careers

An assistant professor at Harvard lives in Cambridge, Massachusetts. Her husband spends most weeks in San Francisco where he works at a popular Internet company. They are both pursuing their careers and so have agreed to spend substantial time apart. She is expecting their first child in a few weeks. I know of several other couples who are or have been in similar situations. Can they sustain such separation? Should they?

Another couple are both scientists. He was offered a singular opportunity for a great job at a prestigious university. She is still a postdoc. She once told me that she was uncomfortable being his "scientific inferior," and preferred that he wait so that they could do the job search together. They are currently separated, due in part to the stress of his new job. Competition between spouses in the professional arena can be particularly stressful for a relationship. This consideration is more important than ever, as more couples today meet in graduate or professional school and have similar career trajectories. I have no personal experience of sharing a profession with my wife. However, it is not difficult to envision some of the problems that can arise. How will I feel if my spouse enjoys more career accolades than I do? How do our career objectives (our definitions of career success) match up? Can I lovingly rejoice in my spouse's achievements as if they were my own, as true agape love would? Can I do so even if I don't achieve as highly? How would my spouse respond to these same questions? If we see potential for danger ahead, what steps will we take to avert it? Can I sacrifice my own ambitions for the sake of the greater blessing of a strong marriage and family life?

The balance between career goals and family goals can be further complicated when both spouses are pursuing careers. However, the process is the same: defining each spouse's career goals, identifying potential conflicts, and deciding how those conflicts will be resolved. Generally, the earlier these discussions occur in a relationship (even before marriage!), the better. Will one spouse stay home with children? Which one, and why? What happens if both spouses find desirable jobs, but in different cities? Whose job takes precedence? As with career-family balance, implementing career-career balance requires a great deal of love and grace from above— particularly when one spouse's career is compromised. A true spirit of grace accepts such sacrifices joyfully for the sake of one's spouse. Our model of spousal sacrifice is Christ himself, for his bride the Church.

Decisions about whether to be a one- or two-income family and about how to manage child care have a huge influence on a family's path and on the childhood experiences of little ones. These decisions are deeply personal and highly dependent on specific circumstances, and discussing them requires special sensitivity. I can think of few things as uncomfortable to me as the implication that I may not be raising my children right. Therefore, regarding this question I would like only to offer a few considerations and questions that entered into the decisions that Rose and I have made. Your loving presence to your children, however much you can offer, is a priceless gift—its value cannot be overestimated. They will not remember how big your home is, how nice your belongings are, or how much stuff you have. But they will remember who took care of them, and they will want to emulate those persons. It is important for children to see their parents do work, but they should not perceive that their parents' work is more important than they are. The raising and education of children is not a second-class occupation, but rather is arguably the most important activity of human society. You are not wasting your education, your talents, or your energy if you devote them to your children, even if you do it full-time. There are options between being a stay-at-home parent and a full-time professional; it's not all-or-nothing. Children will learn everything they learn from other persons. Who will those persons be for your children? If you do decide to give up a career for your children, it is a worthy sacrifice. Finally, children thrive on the routines of life. If your time with your children is limited, make every effort to be there for the rituals and daily routines that you want them to hold in the deepest cores of their being.

Finally, I want to highlight one particular challenge of dual-career couples who do not yet have children. These couples need to be particularly careful to ensure that they spend adequate time together and build their relationship. Too often, it is easy for both spouses to favor work over time spent together, as there are no children involved. Even though Rose does not work outside our home, I know how this situation feels. My laboratory has a happy hour on Friday afternoons, and Rose often brings the boys and joins us. On Friday afternoon, I am always rushing to finish my experiments and projects. Sometimes Rose will call me and let me know that she will be late. When I get that call, I silently rejoice, because it gives me more time to finish my work. I can easily imagine the same call in a two-career marriage: "Sorry, I'm going to be late for dinner." With the pressure off, both husband and wife stay in the office late. They get more work done, but another evening together is lost. (One couple I know solves this problem by making breakfast their "sacred" time to be together!)

5. Vibrant Family Life

As with a successful career, nearly everyone would love to claim a vibrant family life. But, also as with a career, a vibrant family life requires thoughtful planning and sustained effort. Whole books have been devoted to the art of raising a family; here I only wish to touch on a few brief considerations regarding when and why to have children and what constitutes a vibrant family life.

You likely don't need me to list any reasons *not* to start or to grow your family, for they are abundant and, in my experience, often repeated by colleagues and friends. "Stop at two," my current mentor says. "It gets exponentially harder." Some colleagues and friends of mine are waiting for their first "real" job as a professor or at a company; some are waiting for tenure; some for homeownership; some are just enjoying the relative ease and flexibility of a childless marriage. The list of reasons goes on and on.

I also have a number of friends who delayed having children and who now desire to grow or start their families. Many of them are having difficulties conceiving, and some of them even feel a sort of desperation. One friend, a Harvard professor who started his family later in life, has been having difficulty with his wife in conceiving a second child. He intimated to me that, though he has no ethical objections to assisted fertility, the process of seeking fertility treatment is itself uncomfortable, difficult, and stressful for his marriage. He and others who are growing older are facing questions like: am I running out of time to have children? To what lengths will we go in order to conceive? What sort of fertility treatments will we contemplate? What if I am the infertile one? Will my spouse feel that I am letting him or her down? Will raising energetic little children be more difficult now that we're older? After so much time without children, will we be able to adapt our lifestyle to children?

In my experience, most of the reasons that are given for delaying pregnancy fall into just a few categories. One is that children require too much responsibility and would interfere with my other priorities right now. Another is that I don't feel "ready" (with my current job, financial, or living situation) to welcome children. Sometimes such reservations are well justified. However, in many cases, a different attitude can eliminate these fears, help couples to joyfully receive children from the Lord, and bring about a fulfilling family life.

A healthy and life-giving attitude sees children as a gift, indeed the highest gift, of marriage. It begins with a remembrance that the vocation of marriage and family life is a calling from God, and seeks to ask in humble prayer: when does Jesus want us to start our family? How large does He want to grow it? It then views children as a gift freely and joyfully accepted in cooperation with God ("pro-creation"). With the proper attitude, begetting children is not seen as a burden that detracts from our other goals and enterprises, but rather as itself a worthy enterprise to which we eagerly desire to give our time and energy. Indeed, the argument is strong that begetting and raising children is the most worthy of all human enterprises, for its product—the human soul—is designed for eternal life. When we view family life this way, we look forward with joy to its challenges and responsibilities, and our obvious pleasure in raising our children certainly does not go unnoticed by our children or by others.

This understanding of parental responsibility and the accompanying joyful and willing attitude help to guard against the temptation to have children for selfish or unjust reasons. Children are always, without exception, a wonderful gift, but having children because we think they will give meaning to our lives or because having a child is "the thing to do" reflects a truncated understanding that mistakenly puts the focus on the parents. The begetting of a child is a meaningful event, but meaning does not well up from a child and flow into a parent's life. Instead, meaning and love find their source in our relationship with God and overflows from that relationship into the relationship between parents and child. The old saying is true: we can't give what we don't have. We do not imitate our heavenly Father if we beget children so that we can be loved by them. He created us not because our love adds anything to Him, but so that he could "first love us." Parents are called to reflect that same gift of love, pointing our children to the Father of all. It is through parents that children are first taught to pray, to love God and Jesus, and to seek truth, justice, and righteousness. Words are important, but actions even more so.

For a parent, being present to your children and conducting yourself in a worthy manner are both incredibly important for the well-being of children. It may seem patently obvious, but it is also clear from the actions of many that this simple truth is often forgotten. Overwhelming numbers of modern scientific studies are now affirming what generations of parents have known. Children, on average, fare best when they grow up in a household with their married biological parents. A child's family experience—the quality of interactions that a developing child has with his or her primary caregivers and other caring adults, and the nurturing, emotionally responsive environment that adults create—affects a person's outcomes for his or her entire life. In opinion surveys, Americans affirm the value of mothers having more time with children: some 80% of parents agree that staying home or working part-time is better both for young children and for their mothers than full-time work. These data reinforce the idea that parents wield tremendous influence over their children and hence that they bear a grave responsibility to ensure that their children are well cared for.

It is worth noting in this regard that the mere fact that parents are duty-bound to take care of their children does not at all minimize the good works, rendered as to Jesus Himself, that a parent performs each day. For nearly all the spiritual and corporal works of mercy in the Christian tradition are represented in raising children: instructing the ignorant, comforting the sick, clothing the naked, feeding the hungry, giving drink to the thirsty, harboring the harborless, praying for others, bearing wrongs patiently and forgiving offenses willingly. Therefore, one answer to the question, "What can I do to serve Christ in a fuller way?" is to lovingly accept children from the Lord.

Freely willed and joyful acceptance of the gift and responsibility of children, then, is one way to guard against a disordered relationship between career and family. When both family life and career are seen as activities that bring joy and are worthy of our best talents and energies, a natural balance is achieved simply by virtue of this attitude. Notably, such a positive attitude toward rearing children also influences other decisions regarding work and family life. For instance, in my family, my wife, Rose, has elected to stay home with our children because she wants to—she considers it to be such an important task that she wants to give it her own best effort. Similarly, because we were eager to start a family and had children early in our marriage and early in my career, we have established a position of importance for family life in our universe of activities and interactions. My colleagues know that I go home for dinner each night, rarely work on weekends, and seldom travel. In my experience, both my peers and my superiors have come to respect my devotion to my family; I like to think it is because everyone affirms in his heart the importance of family life.

6. Conclusion: final reflections

Our careers and our families are both goods God has given to us that enrich our lives and can bring Him glory. Both are secondary to our relationship with God through Jesus Christ, without whose abundant and undeserved grace we can literally do nothing (not even exist). Neither career nor family is sufficient to fulfill the full range of our human needs. Without work, we cannot provide the basic needs that make family life possible. Without a proper view of family, our spouses and children can suffer unjustly. In the context of a life properly ordered toward God, work and family operate together and constitute the bulk of our life's daily activities. They provide a full range of situations wherein we serve God and others and are ourselves served.

Rose and I strive to uphold a simple rule. When we are making a decision about my career or our family, we duly consider the options and try to choose a path that will be pleasing to God and will, when possible, benefit both aspects of our lives. We seek God's will in prayer together, and if necessary we seek the counsel of holy men and women whom we trust. When it becomes clear that either career or family will significantly suffer for the sake of the other, we have committed to always choose family over career. And we will always say no, with saints like Daniel, to anything that would harm our relationships with God or one another.

My hope is that Christians who are just embarking on promising careers and who are considering marriage or children will pursue both callings with vigor, joy, and love. I hope they will reject the prevalent idea that children detract from a person's other pursuits. In America and in developed countries around the world, our generation is barely—if at all—having enough children to replace itself. The prevailing custom among our most highly educated members of society (we among them) is to focus on their careers during their years of peak fertility, then have smaller families later in life. We often consider attending to children a task best relegated to those whose time is less valuable than our own, so we hire others to do it. Instead of accepting children as a gift from God in accordance with His will, we hire doctors to help us conceive in accordance with our will. Highly educated persons with large families are viewed as anomalies or even fanatics. Aren't large families the business of rednecks and religious freaks?

It need not be so. We can be a generation that affirms the gift of life and welcomes children who grow up secure in the knowledge that they are worth our time, attention, and effort. We can be role models for excellence in our careers and our commitment to our families, and we can promote family-friendly policies in universities and corporations. We even have the ability to make our family lives attractive to others, thus drawing them to the source of all life, Jesus Christ. He has lovingly called many men and women to the sacred and noble vocation of marriage and family life. Others He has called to different vocations. Whatever it be, are we eager to hear and obey His call?

7. Acknowledgments

I am grateful to Rose Cabeen, Imran Babar, Justin Mierzejewski, Martijn Cremers, and Tom Cabeen for helpful discussions and their incisive feedback on drafts of this chapter. Nathan Grills and Soojin Oh provided insightful and careful reviews that greatly improved both the scope and focus of this work. I also thank David Lewis, Nathan Grills, and Josh Swamidass for editing this volume and for encouraging my contribution.

Fitting Faith and Ambition

Bruce R. Huber
Notre Dame Law School
Notre Dame, Indiana
USA

1. Introduction

You are a Christian in a top graduate program. Almost by definition, you are talented, intelligent, motivated, deeply invested in your Christian faith, and generally a "high achiever." Chances are good that this mix of qualities has served you well. By most any measure, you have succeeded and then some.

But chances are also good that you have, at some point along your path of vocational and spiritual development, second-guessed your personal ambition—not the object of that ambition, but the ambition itself. Ambition often presents a stumbling block for followers of Christ, and we approach it with some ambivalence. On the one hand, ambition is the fuel of achievement. Success results in large measure from constant striving and a steadfast determination to perform well in one's pursuits. And Christians' success in worldly affairs can accomplish great good. Our mastery of various domains of knowledge and ability allows us to support our families and our churches, to offer useful goods and services in the marketplace, and perhaps even to cure disease or otherwise alleviate human suffering. Our achievements may bring glory to God and win others to him. Without ambition, Christians passionate for cultural renewal and social change could scarcely attain positions of power and influence.

Furthermore, from a biblical standpoint, ambition might even be regarded as a necessary byproduct of a vibrant relationship with Christ. Consider Paul's exhortation to the Colossians to do all work "as working for the Lord, not for human masters." The Christian's talents are not to be hidden but to be employed for God's purposes, for "from everyone who has been given much, much will be demanded." Surely mediocrity and complacency, in light of teachings such as these, are not what God has in mind for us. Surely excellence and achievement are both gifts from God and goods to which we should aspire in wholehearted pursuit of his best for us. Ambition seems consonant with such aspiration; indeed, the two are indistinguishable.

On the other hand, however, ambition fits only awkwardly with our notions of Christian character. We often find ambition—our own or that of others—distasteful and abrasive, redolent of self-promotion and aggrandizement. The exaltation of self over God and neighbor is, of course, the inversion of the historic Christian ethic. Selfishness is an inevitable manifestation of human fallenness, to be sure, but excessive ambition elevates selfishness into a life strategy. The way of Jesus is one of self-denial, of putting others before self, of humility and not of pride. Are we not taught to choose the least honorable seat at the banquet? that God chooses the humble to shame the wise? that we serve a God who employs the lowly to bring about the grandest of divine accomplishments? "Do nothing out of selfish ambition," warns Paul, "but in humility value others above yourselves." As our Lord spurned rank, prestige, and power (at least of the political or institutional variety), so are his followers right to be wary of worldly advancement, knowing that the goods on offer here pale beside the treasures stored up in heaven.

Moreover, ambition seems symptomatic of a sort of mistaken identity. We sometimes glimpse that those who achieve much have a deep need to achieve much. Their fear of insignificance, of being average, is a strong and awful motive force. Their identity consists of the sum of their accomplishments. Failure presents an existential threat. Ambition is the visible crust atop the tectonic plates of ego and insecurity that drive their behavior. And we who easily diagnose this pathology in others' ambition? If we are honest, we are troubled by their self-adulation in large part because we would prefer that attention and recognition were showered on us. We are never so quick to condemn ambition as when its bearer is stealing the acclaim we believe is rightly ours. All of this, of course, is contra our shared identity as children of God. Hopefully we are fortunate enough every so often to be blessed with a bit of Ecclesiastical wisdom and to remember just how inconsequential are our puny affairs, and how foolishly we imagine them to justify our existence.

Such are the roots of our ambivalence over ambition. Most of the time, this ambivalence is a gnat easily batted away.

But it deserves closer inspection if only for those moments at which it is at its most acute. Doubt about the propriety of ambition can strike a particularly sensitive nerve in those accustomed to accomplishment and achievement. Our striving, our disciplined labor, our hard work, and our incessant desire for success—are they improper? The very possibility calls into question not only our prior behavior but our current pursuits and our future trajectory.

So what to make of ambition? In this brief essay, I wish to offer several modest (unambitious?) reflections on the Christian's relationship to ambition. I begin with the unremarkable, even pat suggestion that our reflections about ambition ought to be oriented around God's redemptive work, enacted in Christ, rather than around our moral improvement. Thus grounded, we begin to see that the problem of ambition is really a special case of the problem of Christian identity, as it presents among those of us whose self-conception is largely shaped by professional accomplishment. For us in particular, it is important to remember, as a matter of discipline, that the Christian's identity is not strictly individual but corporate and communal as well. The development of the body of Christ is served by individual ambition when such ambition amplifies gifts that nurture and sustain the church. Furthermore, ambition of this sort is a central manifestation of the freedom purchased for us by Christ. The freedom to work, to create, to thrive in God's creation is augmented by ambition calibrated to God's purposes. The service of God, then, is not antithetical to our individual ambition and achievement, but subsumes it within the augmentation of his kingdom.

2. Ambition: Good, Bad … or Wrong Question?

As a threshold matter, we would do well to resist the impulse to render a simplistic, final moral judgment: "ambition is good" or "ambition is sinful." Only a tiny sliver of human behavior may be disposed of so straightforwardly, yet a hallmark of contemporary Christian culture is the urgency with which it seeks (and delivers) binary moral pronouncements on matters of great complexity. Unmoored from the historic anchors of reformed theology, which rightly emphasize God's salvific work over human moral striving, everyday Christianity has accepted, if only gradually and without formal acknowledgment, an inadequate and inaccurate conception of human sinfulness. Sin is widely treated as a set of particular acts or omissions to be dodged as if on an obstacle course. Navigate the course; remain free from sin. "All these commandments I have kept since my youth," we aspire to boast, with the young lawyer before Jesus.

Sin is not like that. Sin is a condition that, although it manifests in particular conduct, does not consist in that conduct; it consists in the human heart's constant rebellion from God. "The Lord saw that every inclination of man's heart was only evil all the time"(Gen 6:5). This is not to say that moral judgment is impossible or that moral reflection is not worthwhile; it is only to say that our compulsion to denominate particular actions as good/bad stems from a problematic theological root.

This compulsion is particularly problematic in thinking about ambition, because the consequence of reaching the wrong conclusion may be serious. If we tend to think of ambition as appropriate, we run the risk that we will fail to take seriously the real dangers associated with the pursuit of worldly benefits and advantages. If we tend to think of ambition as sinful, we may not only neglect the gifts that God has given us, but also begrudge him our imagined restriction, wishing that we could be free to pursue the goals and aims that come most naturally to us. Many times I have come across young Christian students who operate on the assumption that God's will and their own ambitions are necessarily at odds. I think it unwise to assume such a zero-sum situation. There is every reason to believe that God designed humans to enjoy implementing and employing the capabilities that he gave us and that make us human. To be sure, the distortive force of sin corrupts our ambitions, but within God's common grace exists the possibility that our aspirational inclinations bear his imprint. It is something like this idea that must undergird Frederick Buechner's famous claim that, "Vocation is the place where our deep gladness meets the world's deep need."

A thoughtful Christian posture toward ambition, then, should be grounded in Christianity's central affirmation that God has acted in Christ to save his people and to redeem his creation. Moral striving neither saves us nor wins us favor with God. In seeking to sort right from wrong, we act in gratitude to God and seek a deep consistency with his redemptive work, in keeping with our eternal calling. Indeed, it is no accident that such a basis for moral reflection provides rich soil for appropriate human ambition. Obedience to God—grounded in gratitude, empowered by his grace, and impelled by the biblical vision of creation's redemption—does not rule out ambition, but redirects it by placing Christ at the center of our aspiration. If the worship, proclamation, and exaltation of Christ are at the heart of our ambition, the risks that attend worldly achievement take on a different character.

3. Placing Christ at the Center of Our Ambition

It would be conclusory at this point to offer the facile observation that ambition in the service of God and others is fine, but ambition in the service of self is wrong. Such a characterization slips right back into binary moral judgment, of which we have just spoken, and also merely begs the question. What does it mean for ambition to be centered in Christ? How on earth could one deploy such an idea in real pursuits in the real world? After all, the conceptual grid within which we normally deal with ambition is a professional careerist one, marked by the conventional milestones of academic or professional achievement. How does that grid intersect with the One True Grid, the biblical grid on which God's designs for creation play out?

To ask that question is almost to answer it. If there is such a thing as One True Grid—one meta-narrative that spans time and place—then to live life off-grid, that is, without regard to God, is to waste one's life. "They followed worthless idols and themselves became worthless." It is not worth sugar-coating here. To center our ambition on Christ requires the hard and constant work of centering, the disciplined summoning to the forefront of our minds that "I am not my own, but belong, body and soul, in life and in death, to my faithful savior, Jesus Christ." To affirm this truth is not to denigrate our daily affairs, our careers, and such, or to back away from what has earlier been said about our aspirations bearing his imprint. But fitting faith and ambition requires an understanding of our true identity, both individually and corporately, and the shape of the freedom that our identity in Christ provides.

3.1 Ambition and Identity

We have already suggested that much of what troubles us about ambition has to do with identity. In fact, we might even say that ambition poses only a superficial challenge, because it is generally not ambition per se that troubles us. It is instead such qualities as self-promotion, self-aggrandizement, vanity, undue pride, and the like—qualities that signify deep insecurity, that desperately cry out, "I matter!" Ambition is often their consort, and thus ambition in the service of self is pathetic or even repulsive; yet ambition in the service of something else, or someone else, is benign at worst and inspiring at best. We are drawn toward, for example, those athletes who seem motivated by bringing joy to others or by team rather than individual success—in stark contrast to the histrionic juvenility so prevalent in professional sports (except baseball). In the academic realm, we are not put off by scholars who genuinely pursue knowledge in the service of the public interest—in stark contrast to the absurd and trivial squabbles that are so commonplace in academia, transparently rooted in ego, insecurity, and reputational micromanagement.

Yet for many of us, our identity—our self-definition—is wrapped up in career and accomplishment. In part, this is just a cultural convention; even in mundane settings, we routinely describe each other by our professions almost as routinely as we exchange names. "I'd like you to meet John; he's an accountant." More deeply, though, by our attitudes and actions we manifest an astonishingly persistent preoccupation with professional status. We not uncommonly—and I speak from personal experience here—blow certain objectives and achievements out of all proportion, as though our very lives would end (or worse, our reputations collapse) should tenure or such-and-such a grant or award not come to pass.

Since Sunday school we have been taught that we have an identity of far greater importance than our worldly accomplishments, nay, than any external descriptor. If "I am not my own, but belong to my faithful savior, Jesus Christ," this fact defines us more completely and authentically than any other. We are the very children of God, beloved by him and purchased at great price; we ought see ourselves and each other as God himself sees us, clothed in Christ's righteousness, and of intrinsic and inestimable value simply because of our status as his children. From this simple truth, or something not too far from it, flow the most profound reflections on human equality that political philosophy has yet produced. This truth about who we really are ought by rights to dwarf our self-doubts and insecurities. Of course, it is not only the accomplished who forget who they are. In a host of respects, Christians forfeit the freedom that could come from a wholehearted embrace of the identity bestowed upon them by God. Misguided ambition is simply one outgrowth of a failure to appropriate completely the idea that one is made in the image of God, offered salvation from him apart from any individual merit, and loved and accepted as his child on the same grounds.

3.2 Ambition and Community

Just as important as our individual identity as children of God is our corporate identity as members of the church. In fact, it is our membership in the church, and our participation in it, that is most likely to provide the antidote to our individual obsessions with accomplishment. It is in the community of faith that we partake of the sacraments, hear the preaching of the Word, and are given the opportunity to step outside the work-week and regain a broader view of our life and purpose. But our membership in the church does more than correct our misdirection; it also provides a new basis for ambition. The biblical idea of the church as the "body of Christ" offers a different paradigm for thinking about one's talents and achievements.

The texts that speak of the church as Christ's body employ that metaphor not only to emphasize our fundamental unity (and the absurdity of division), but also to explain and contextualize our innate differences. The twelfth chapter of Paul's first letter to the Corinthians speaks directly to this point. Just as the various parts of the human body are diverse and specialized, so also each member of the church has different gifts and consequently a different role and function. Each member is called upon to employ his or her gifts for the service of the entire body ("for the common good"). Importantly, the body functions best when each of its parts are healthy and effective. Weakness or injury in one organ can impair or disable the entire body.

The implications of this metaphor for our present discussion are profound. First, our utter dependence on the rest of the body is revealed; gone is any basis for arrogance or self-promotion on account of our particular gifts or abilities. As Paul writes to the Romans:

Do not think of yourself more highly than you ought, but rather think of yourself with sober judgment, in accordance with the measure of faith God has given you. Just as each of us has one body with many members, and these members do not all have the same function, so in Christ we who are many form one body, and each member belongs to all the others. We have different gifts, according to the grace given us.

Second, however, ambition is cast in a wholly different light. We see that ambition is not merely acceptable or tolerable but vital insofar as it serves the well-being of the body as a whole, and is implemented in coordination with the rest of the body. Striving for excellence and attainment is nonsensical if the goal is personal aggrandizement, but nourishing and fortifying if the goal is the good of the body.

Consider Paul once more. The apostle denigrates his pedigree and accomplishments to the extent that they might give rise to "confidence in the flesh," and yet his letters reflect a clear and remarkably focused ambition. Paul is not shy about emphasizing the basis of his apostleship, asserting his leadership, or correcting errors among the churches. He does not back away from the role given him, and declares that he "strains toward what is ahead, pressing on toward the goal." He manifests what we must characterize as "ambition," but does so in furtherance of the cause of Christ as a direct, not indirect, objective. And importantly, Paul's understanding of his role within the church includes his awareness that weakness, far from undermining confidence in one's calling, allows Christ's power to be displayed as the motive force behind the movements of the body.

Thus a focus on the body of Christ does not squelch individual drive or progress. Quite the contrary. The corporate view situates and right-sizes individual accomplishment by bluntly analogizing it with individual body parts and functions. Ambition of the self-serving variety severs an organ from the body. That organ can only wither and die. But a properly functioning organ owes a constant duty of top performance, in a sense, to the rest of the body.

3.3 Ambition and Freedom

This duty to the rest of the body is one source of the biblical admonition to do all work "as working for the Lord." To conceive of ambition as a sort of duty to others is a bit jarring. In this section, I wish to explore this duty and link it to the idea of freedom.

Duty suggests a limitation of freedom. We generally understand freedom in terms of the absence of constraint, but another important aspect of freedom has to do with development. One who is not fully developed lacks a basic form of freedom. A toddler is not free to play baseball, by which I mean that the toddler simply lacks the skills and capabilities required to play the game. It is through development that the toddler may acquire the requisite skills. That process of development will most likely involve (perhaps even require) disciplined practice and repeated effort—in a sense, the imposition of constraints, as opposed to their absence. The process will be aided by the child's ambition to become a good ballplayer.

Similarly, our freedom to become fully functioning members of the body of Christ involves development, and that development is aided by our ambition to serve the church—to discharge our duty to her—to the greatest extent possible. In this sense, it is through the disciplined nurture of our God-given gifts that we attain to the freedom that is our inheritance in Christ. Ambition in the service of the body of Christ leads us toward a passion for serving the church to the best of our abilities. Are you a high-achiever? Employ your gifts as best you can—and develop them wholly—to the good of the people of God. As you grow and mature you will become more free, not less, to serve the body of Christ.

I do not mean here to place us back under the "yoke of the law" against which John Calvin inveighed when addressing the nature of Christian liberty. I mean only to suggest a connection between ambition, duty, and freedom. Why is the connection important to this discussion? Because freedom is something of a fixation in contemporary culture, both within the church and without; in my estimation, a proper understanding of ambition augments and enriches our understanding of genuine human freedom. Freedom concerns not only our soteriological status (closer to Calvin's concern) but also our range of action. The aspiration to serve the church more fully and completely expands our range of action, and allows us to take in more of the very gift of human life. We thrive in God's creation when "we live and move and have our being" in him, free to enjoy all that he has given us and all that he is made—precisely because he has, by grace, developed us and endowed us with the capacity to enjoy him and the world he has made. God-given freedom includes the freedom to aspire.

4. Conclusion

In these respects, we see how it is possible for ambition to arise as a consequence of, rather than a possible competitor to, obedience to Christ. This is quite a different view of ambition from the one that we normally hold, or at least the one with which I am intimately familiar. It is not a perspective that comes particularly naturally. So we would do well to think carefully about ambition in this way, rather than reject or condemn it, knee-jerk, or assume that it is necessarily self-oriented. We would do well to remember our true identity—as God's beloved children and as members of his church—because ambition sourced elsewhere corrupts the beauty of our giftedness and renders it immaterial. We would do well, in short, as a matter of personal discipline, to place Christ and his church at the center of our ambition.

Success: Whose Will is Being Done?

Nathan Grills
University of Melbourne
Australia

1. Introduction

"Our father in heaven, hallowed be my name,
My kingdom come, my will be done on earth as it is in heaven.
I can earn my daily bread. For the kingdom the power and the
glory are mine, now and forever, amen"

I would guess that the world in which Christian professionals and academics live would be far more comfortable with
the above paraphrased version of the Lord's prayer than the
actual Lord's prayer. This distortion reflects the values that are
revered in our secular society – ambition, wealth, power and
self-advancement – and the success in attaining these determines one's own ultimate value. Although the initial response
as a Christian would be to see such a mantra as being conceited and self-centered there is a temptation for those of us
who claim to follow Jesus' teaching, to act in ways consistent
with this distortion.

I choose to begin this chapter with this prayer because it highlights the tension that many Christians face in striving for success in various academic and professional fields. Many Christians in academia strive to faithfully use (or the preferred Christian term 'to steward') the gifts that God has given them. It follows, particularly in the evangelical discourse, that success may result from such stewardship. However, in this process, how do we keep God's will central and hallow His name when the environment in which we work promotes seeking success for one's own glory and so that our name will be hallowed? That might sound trite, but most of us in professional and academic roles know that success breeds success. Therefore, bringing credibility to one's own name, referred to by employment consultants as building your personal brand, will help with the next publication, the next grant, the next academic grade, and, eventually, tenure at Harvard, or another esteemed Ivy League university. For example, a single publication in Nature will see your name hallowed and will endear you to selection committees forever more. It is perhaps ironic that the premise of getting this book published is that known names are publishable names.

Seeking recognition of our work in order to advance our work and career is not necessarily wrong. However, where the intent and outcome is for our glory and prestige, we must challenge ourselves by asking which prayer we are praying? Are we more interested in success, not for God's glory, but in order to construct an identity and prove our adequacy through personal achievement? This can be associated with a lack of real experience of our identity, or our deeper meaning, being founded in Christ alone. Granted, God allows us to create our unique individuality from various sources, including our work and successes. 'Christ alone' implies that our deeper or deepest meaning and purpose are derived from Christ. In comparison to this ultimate meaning all other things are worthless. Perhaps a litmus test is failure? When we aren't recognized, which will happen to even the most successful and accomplished professor on occasions, do feelings of inadequacy cause despair?

This chapter further explores the ideas of success and failure and how we, as Christians and professionals or academics, might approach these faithfully. I start by exploring the issue of identity and the *drug of success,* and then consider how disability and failure can be a severe mercy for successful Christians. The chapter draws on my personal life experience. An important caveat is that these reflections are from a professional and academic still struggling through the very real tensions involved in remaining faithful at work.

2. In Christ Alone

In 1962 the then Warden of Rhodes House, Edgar Williams, summed up the psychological process that a Rhodes Scholar elect goes through:

"When he (sic.) is first awarded the Scholarship, the successful scholar's reaction is nearly always that there must have been a mistake; he cannot possibly possess the semi-divine attributes which Rhodes demanded in his elect. Next comes the realization that no mistake has been made: Quite a lot of fuss is made of him, particularly locally, and he comes to regard himself as a very remarkable chap, although in most cases he keeps his head about it. Finally he arrives at Oxford, still conscious of his glory, and finds, in some cases to his surprise, that he is of no importance at all, and the one thing Oxford requires of these leaders of tomorrow is that they should not start leading today."

Many of my fellow scholars can remember the first Oxford winter and the feelings of being "of no importance at all." Along with many of my peers I was suffering from what I termed Rhodes Scholar Syndrome. Or maybe Rhodes Scholar Seasonal Affective Disorder would be a better description, given that the bleak British winter would make even those of the strongest constitution question whether life was worthwhile! Whatever the name, after the adrenaline of Michaelmas-term subsided and the bleak mid-winter set in, so did the intense experience of worthlessness. Feelings of low self-esteem and inadequacy plagued me during the depth of winter and I owe it to my wife, Claire, and my church, St Ebbes, for helping me through.

I came to realize that I wasn't alone, and this sickness was nearly universal amongst Rhodes Scholars *coming up* to Oxford. Common to many scholars were personal characteristics of low self-esteem or feelings of inadequacy, which had become a powerful motivating force. These had proven a harsh taskmaster and driven many of these young students, all less than twenty-five years old, to prove their worth to themselves and to others, through achievement in all areas of their lives. Achieve they had done: culminating in being awarded perhaps the world's most prestigious academic scholarship. So counter-intuitively, this group of prestigious scholars were some of the most insecure. They had the self-esteem of 'a kettle boiled dry,' as a friendly Yorkshireman put it.

I wasn't the first 'successful' Christian to go through this experience, nor is this syndrome unique to Rhodes Scholars (successful is in inverted commas to reflect a worldly and shallow definition of success). And the problem is not confined to our modern highly professionalized world where many evangelical Christian scholars have opportunities to 'succeed.' As I read the Bible and sing old hymns I realize that there were many before me for whom 'success' was a profoundly empty experience. Insightful hymns, Paul's letters, Psalms and Ecclesiastes are all testimony to the fact that far greater people than I have struggled with this throughout the ages. Having achieved success they became aware of how that success may have given them an identity but not true meaning. For others in the Bible it took failure to highlight the fact that success had become an idol for them. The repentance of these saints is recorded in Scripture, psalms and songs.

This problem of attempting to find one's deeper meaning in success (wisdom, money, family) is so clearly and beautifully narrated in Ecclesiastes. The entire book of Ecclesiastes reflects a yearning for deeper meaning. The writer turns to success, wealth, wisdom, exquisite culinary experience, but all such earthly achievements are found wanting. They are, as the author vividly states, "a chasing after the wind," and they are all vanities that are "here today and gone tomorrow." The New Testament is also replete with references to the importance of finding our meaning in Christ alone...and to counting all but loss compared to the greatness of knowing Christ Jesus our Lord. As Galatians 6:14 says: "May I never boast but in the Cross of Christ."

For the Christian in a vocational or academic role, our identity and purpose must be found in Christ, not in what we do. I am so often tempted to measure my adequacy by my achievement and by what others think and not what God thinks. Vaughan Roberts, my vicar at the church I attended while studying in Oxford, gave me the standard prescription that he had given to many other students at Oxford struggling with low self-esteem and inadequacy: a daily reading of Psalm 62:1-2 (NIV):

"My soul finds rest in God alone; my salvation comes from him. He alone is my rock and my salvation; he is my fortress, I will never be shaken…"

This has been helpful and for many years I've let my mind return to this Scripture when my academic identity is threatened by self-doubt and external critique that tempted me to despair.

As I struggled through this 'Syndrome,' the words of a number of hymns have challenged me, and made me realize that my Christian forbears have also shared my anguish. The words of 'Be Thou my Vision' ring so true and I am sure the author, over a 1000 years ago, was experiencing the same temptation to find his identity in something other than Christ:

"Riches I heed not or man's empty praise,
Thou mine inheritance now and always"

Likewise, I imagine that Isaac Watts had being struggling with seeking his identity in vain things when he penned the stirring hymn "When I Survey the Wondrous Cross":

"Forbid it, Lord, that I should boast,
Save in the death of Christ my God!
All the vain things that charm me most,
I sacrifice them to His blood"

Of course, God expects us to take responsibility for our own giftedness, and to make good use of the assets he has given us for His service. However, the basis for *succeeding faithfully* is being sure of our primary identity in Christ ... alone. If we find our primary value and worth elsewhere then we set ourselves up for failure in our vocation and more importantly failure in our Christian witness. A shaky identity in Christ leads to a striving for worldly success for our own glory and not God's. It leads to a desire to be accepted and respected for the great things we can achieve in our earthly lives.

When our ultimate meaning is derived from Christ alone, as my vicar Vaughan recognized, then who I am is no longer determined by what I achieve. It is not a major revelation for the Christian who has sung the words, recited creeds and told fellow believers that our value is in Christ, not in worldly success. I am assuming that, as discerning and intelligent readers, I do not need to reinforce this knowledge to you. But, oh how I struggle with that on a daily, if not hourly, basis. So for me, every reminder from the Bible, from hymns, from my vicar, from my friends and even from my mum is a welcome challenge to me. Vaughan knew the perfect verses to give to me to help me through the darkness of Rhodes' Scholar Syndrome. May my soul continue to "find rest in God alone as He alone is my rock and my salvation"!

So why are we tempted to measure our careers according to the values of the world such as tenure, salary and success?

Why do we chase after such things? Well, success fills, how-ever temporarily, the gap left from an incomplete awareness of our value in Christ. It is almost as if we become emotion-ally and psychologically addicted to the success drug. It's a quick hit and we all know how gratifying it feels. Whereas other illicit drugs kill the body, the success drug can kill the heart and soul. When we gravitate toward finding our sense of meaning in our success, in work or ministry, then we are on the path to self-destruction. When unchecked, success becomes our identity, and can destroy us. Like the athlete's success brought about by anabolic steroids, it is ultimately self-defeating. What price are we prepared to pay?

From our earliest days we are groomed to seek the quick hit of success. It brings instant rewards and approval from every-one we care for: Mum, Dad, teachers and friends. Success is cause for celebration: hugs and cheers of delight ensue after you take your first steps! The childhood memories that stand out are the memories of success such as the image of myself at a school sports day, wearing an orange T-shirt (the school colors), covered with blue ribbons. This image, like others cap-turing success, is preserved in photos. Tennis trophies adorned my childhood bedroom and I spent hours admiring them and wanting to, no, needing to, add to them. Juvenile Rheumatoid Arthritis threatened my ability to succeed physically but other forms of the success drug were readily available. I success-fully chased after academic scholarships, youth of the year, theatre school colors and more.

My dear Gran was a close and treasured friend, and I viv-idly remember running to tell my Gran of each success and achievement. She would be so proud and immediately tell me to go and ring my dear Aunt Mary. She would be equally thrilled. It is great that we celebrate each other's earthly successes but I can't remember ringing her to tell her I'd become a Christian. Likewise I don't remember ringing her to tell her that I lost my tennis match, that the experience was enjoyable, that I played for the glory of God, or that I made my competitors really happy by losing. Parents, and even Christian parents, don't really reward those things. So why would a kid strive after them? What of my sister, whose disability meant she never achieved the same successes as her brothers? I know she felt inferior and undervalued by Gran.

Then there was admission to medical school, dux of medical school and a Rhodes Scholarship. I think that at a young age I became addicted to the pleasure that success brought. However, perhaps it is those who keep succeeding who are most in danger of addiction. Nothing succeeds like success. There is an insidious reinforcement loop at work which is highly seductive. For this there is not a drug test! Yet God, in his grace, often has a way of showing up our positive drug-test. Although He may use our conscience, our friends, our family or community, it seems that He is most effective at using our failures. For, as Keller describes it, when our counterfeit god is threatened, then the resultant despair reveals that what might be a good thing, such as success, has become an ultimate thing. Withdrawal, when it happens, destroys this counterfeit god and leaves nothing except room for critical reflection. Unfortunately, those who are successful have these experiences too rarely and can be fooled into thinking that they can maintain a constant supply of success from now into eternity.

It was whilst I was at Oxford that I experienced withdrawal and subsequent brokenness and it was precipitated when my identity was threatened. As the wise warden of Rhodes House had alluded to in 1962: having many successful people around me made me feel very insignificant. The success hit became harder to find as I found I was actually not that bright. This withdrawal experience, as explained earlier, prompted a kind of second conversion experience as I plumbed the depths of my heart and saw that it was empty. It was in my failure to achieve that God chose to speak to me.

3. Grey, the Color of Success

When I began my DPhil at Oxford, it seemed entirely consistent with my faith and where God was leading me in my life. And it was only after much prayer and discernment that I decided to stay on in Oxford after completing my masters to complete the DPhil. By God's design I was able to research the effect of faith in the response of faith-based groups to HIV in India. It was clear how this DPhil would prepare us to follow our calling to work with faith based groups in India. The opportunity to undertake such research at a leading largely secular university with supervisors who were internationally recognized in the Public Health arena could have only been a God thing!

Yet as I strived to complete this successfully and quickly - so I could return to India and begin serving God there – this worthy goal imperceptibly became an addiction to succeeding. If this was an insidious process, then it was my monthly supervisor meetings that made the diagnosis clear. Each criticism from my supervisor (and as most who have done doctorates know there tends to be many at supervisor meetings) pene-trated deeply and gave rise to deep self-doubt. The DPhil had become more than just a piece of academic work and was actually becoming who I was. The thought that "I just can't do this" haunted me as I think I was afraid that my meaning in life, my DPhil, would fail and I would be exposed as one big fraud: totally inadequate, hopeless. A failure in the world's eyes. It was at the Harvey Fellowship Summer Institute that I was really convicted that the greyness had become black! At this forum we spent time exploring issues of Christian ambi-tion and success and it convicted me that the desire to succeed and the desire to find my identity in a completed DPhil was leading me to compromise. How stupid! It was about as in-congruous as a Christian stealing a Bible to get closer to God! I was doing this DPhil because God had ordained it, and I was doing it for God's glory, but an obsession with succeeding was even leading me to compromise my academic integrity. This realization and the repentance that ensued led me to significantly rewrite my DPhil to exclude any misrepresenta-tions, half-truths and embellished conclusions.

Success need not displace God or become our purpose for living. It is not wrong to strive to successfully serve God, to successfully complete a project, to successfully lead a minis-try, or to successfully lead a company, organization or research collaboration. In fact, taking such a role could be good stew-ardship of the resources and skills God has entrusted to you. However, whilst achieving is not sinful itself, the motivation to achieve *is*, if it replaces the centrality of God in our lives. Again, one can't overemphasize how surreptitiously success can become our god: a drug that we begin to depend on.

Perhaps I might further illustrate this with an example from my personal experience as a young Christian doctor who watched many other young Christian doctors struggle with their faith. Many of these Christian doctors entered medical school with the idea of using their skills to serve God and contribute to Kingdom work by serving and reaching out to those in need. After graduation, conceit swells. The young doctor now holds lives in his hand, and is warmly appreciated by staff and patients. Material success is alluring, and adulation is intoxicating. The satisfaction of playing God can very easily replace the God we were aiming to serve. Perhaps this partly explains why some of my Christian colleagues have slowly lost any place for God. It was never a conscious decision but it was just that they no longer sensed a need for Him in their lives. Their success, and the control and power it gave, had displaced God.

Even those in ministry, or maybe I should say especially those in ministry, will attest to the grey area whereby success in ministry can itself become what we serve. Jesus' teaching on the Lord's Prayer is actually about religious people understanding the real motives behind righteous acts: in this case giving, praying and fasting (Matthew 6 vv 16-18). Often our motives start out as pure, but most ministry by its very nature, is noticed and often revered. How quickly the motive can grow for another hit of being noticed, appreciated and affirmed! As a Christian overseas worker I strive to serve God successfully, and our work, by God's grace, has been successful. And success requires promoting our work and encouraging others to become involved and also financially support this work. However, I am only too aware of the blurred line whereby having to promote the work (i.e. have it noticed) blurs to grey and becomes addictive. The success of gaining people's support is a tremendous boost to the ego. Sometimes I need to take a step back and ask if my identity has become entwined in being a successful missionary, and promoting my name, rather than my identity being grounded in God's will and hallowing His name. At times I have crossed the line and begun to serve the serving of God rather than serving God Himself. When Jesus teaches us how to pray, it is in the context of warning about not doing acts of righteousness to be noticed. This is pertinent to us professional Christians as we strive to succeed. We must be cognizant that it is His name we hallow and His kingdom we invoke – not our own!

I think that many of us exist day-to-day and year-to-year in the grey area in between hallowing His name and hallowing our name. So how do we faithfully succeed? The more I think about how difficult succeeding faithfully is, the more I question if it is really possible for a 'successful' person to stay faithful. Maybe this is overstating it, but the parable about the rich man comes to mind and I wonder if it also applies to the successful man. Is it just as hard for a successful man to enter the kingdom of God as it is for a rich man? Matthew 19:21-24 (NIV) says:

"Jesus answered, "If you want to be perfect, go, sell your possessions and give to the poor, and you will have treasure in heaven. Then come, follow me." When the young man heard this, he went away sad, because he had great wealth." Then Jesus said to his disciples, "I tell you the truth, it is hard for a rich man to enter the kingdom of heaven. Again I tell you, it is easier for a camel to go through the eye of a needle than for a rich man to enter the kingdom of God."

I am not saying that we go away sad, because we have great success or that success is incompatible with Christian life. Even though this passage throws out a searching challenge, it also has its gracious consolation. With God, everything is possible (vs 26). But I think we need to be prepared, if God so asks, to sacrifice it all. While it may be radically counter-cultural, there will be times in our career that being faithful will mean being a broken and unsuccessful person! Being faithful might mean refusing a promotion in order to protect our family, for example, or devote time to church, or speak into the lives of those at work. Granted, being faithful might not always give you the instant hit that being successful might. Yet we are not called to be successful, only faithful. Somehow the two terms - success and faith - have become dangerously conflated in contemporary evangelicalism. However, successful people can be very unfaithful. It's harder for such a person to depend on God. As already discussed, perhaps they are successful because of a deep drive to find their identity in their secular success rather than in God.

On a number of occasions I have been asked to speak to large numbers of people because I am a "successful Christian." However, I think that phrase "successful Christian" needs unpacking. In the world's eyes I might be successful but does that qualify me to give a testimony at a large Christian convention? Does that qualify me to be a church elder? Probably not! Perhaps our Christian leaders do us disservice when they select people more on the basis of their earthly success than spiritual maturity. It is one thing to be successful and a Christian but that is quite different from being successful in our Christian walk. After all, the definition of success for the Christian is about bringing glory to God in all we do...and that could mean being an absolute failure in the world's eyes.

4. Disability, a Severe Mercy for the Successful

If the successful have to live in this grey area, then what I am learning from my two-year-old daughter is that she has it all worked out: black and white! In a life where worldly success is unlikely, given her disability – and is no longer even a thought we focus on - my daughter is teaching me that being faithful is foremost. Interestingly I think her condition will also make me a better father of my "normal" boy. I have learned that celebrating worldly success, while not wrong, will be comparatively unimportant compared with celebrating who my son is: created in the image of God and loved by Him.

The Power of the Powerless, by De Vink, is a challenging book whereby Mr. De Vink outlines just how transformative was the experience of having a brother with profound mental and physical disability. He was a complete failure when looking through the eyes of the world. Henri Nouwen in the introduction to this book describes how disability challenges our conceited, and often selfish, ideas of success. He writes that,

"In a world that so much wants to control life and decide what is good, healthy, important, valuable and worthwhile, this book makes the shocking observation that what is hidden from the "learned and clever" is revealed to mere children."

The disabled challenge us to see our value and success differently.

This Easter I was asked to speak at a convention about our work in India. Doubtlessly they wanted to hear about our ministry successes but I felt led to speak about disability and our personal experience of it. It was so fulfilling to be able to take Abby's illness, unpack it in the scheme of God's eternal purposes, and then share this with 2500 people. The joy I took in this opportunity was right. The encouragement that my story was to others was right. Wasn't it great that God allowed me to see his purposes in Abby's illness for my professional work with the University of Melbourne, for our mission in North India and for my personal life? Hmmm. I wonder.

The talk was well received and as I sat down in my seat I was content that I had delivered the talk with compassion, emotion and impact. Although the success of the talk was good, even in this situation I could feel the temptation to seek my sense of identity from achieving in this different way. I liked the attention that this talk had brought to our worthy work... and even to our situation. That feeling of significance that I had from 'doing' all this was not far below the surface. And, the appreciation of 2500 people brings a warm inner glow.

I sat there and pondered my own heart in delivering this talk. Sure, I wanted to share Abby's story, as I knew it would challenge people both personally and to serve cross culturally. But even here there were mixed motivations. I looked across at Abby, sitting on my wife's knee. In a strange way, she was free from the 'something' that Nouwen refers to when he speaks about the liberation of working in disability. I wondered about the something that "keeps pulling me back to the place of success and praise." That something was perhaps my mixed motivations, and I wrote down on the service running sheet as I reflected on my feelings:

"Abby is everything that I am not. She brings glory to God without mixed motives. She doesn't care what others think. She doesn't strive for success in the world's eyes or to be recognized. She brings glory to Him and not to herself. She brings glory to Him in her weakness not her accomplishments. She doesn't get her value or meaning from anything except Christ...Christ alone."

Abby's witness was not, and will not, be greyed with mixed motivations of success, significance in achievements or an identity based in her successful work.

A conversation with a friend after the meeting made me think that my experience of God would be diminished if there were only successful professionals worshipping God in this auditorium. The weak often point people to God's power and experience God in ways different from the successful. My friend, a new believer and a successful manager at a leading firm, observed the various expressions of weakness in the room and commented condescendingly "are we the only normal ones in this place?" I thought long and hard about this and what came to mind was Paul's teaching in 1 Corinthians 1: 27-29 (NIV):

"But God chose the foolish things of the world to shame the wise; God chose the weak things of the world to shame the strong. He chose the lowly things of this world and the despised things—and the things that are not—to nullify the things that are, so that no one may boast before him."

Yes, there were a whole lot of different, broken, weak and "foolish" people in this room. After my talk a number of them came to tell me about their experiences of weakness: a mother who had failed to cure her 15-year-old daughter of an aggressive brain tumor, a father of a severely disabled boy whose career has been ruined, a woman who failed in her career, a missionary who failed in his mission due to illness, a lady who had failed in her marriage. But their faith shamed the worldly wisdom of my friend. The depth of identity found in Christ through one's failures and weakness, as opposed to one's successes, brings authenticity to the Christian walk. Brokenness in our midst leads to an awareness of our need for God, and an awareness that our real identity is in Christ alone.

In that same meeting, down the front row, I observed a boy with Down's syndrome dancing around and worshipping God like a fool! Actually it is me who was the fool...he was really "shaming the wise" in that room! He didn't care, like I did, what people thought: he just wanted to praise God and he did it so beautifully. If only we could have faith like a child... or, even better, faith like a child with an intellectual disability! Disability and weakness in our midst encourages us to be ourselves with our vulnerabilities and inadequacies. Although it is not wrong to be successful /cool/accepted/strong I don't think we have to be and it is a risk to strive to be! We are successful in Christ alone.

Disability has forced me to focus on His Kingdom, His will and His glory because my kingdom, my will and my glory are in tatters. Abby isn't aware of it but her life is playing out in a way that promotes this rethink. Our preconceived plans for Abby's life and our long term ministry plans have been laid aside, but His will for Abby is still perfect. Maybe, just maybe, disability (in which I include vulnerability, weakness, brokenness and failure) is the solution to realigning our vocation with God's will, glory and kingdom.

5. The Fallible Faithful

I hope this chapter might have prompted introspection about both the dangers of success and the importance of failure. So what should we expect now? Is the experience of failure somehow protective against the drug of success? I don't think so. I haven't been protected. As we continue to use our gifts for His glory, and at times experience success, we need to realize that we will time and again find ourselves in the grey area in which our achievement has become our primary calling, and we are motivated for our glory, kingdom, will and purpose. I suggest that for faithful Christians this may occur multiple times in a career, a year ...or even in a day! When successful persons claim to succeed for God's glory, kingdom, or name alone then they are deluded and lacking self-awareness about their intractable mixed motives. The idea of believing that we have succeeded in 'succeeding faithfully' is in itself an arrogance that puts one is at risk of spiritual death. Perhaps only after our physical death will we reach such purity of motivation, when we rest in Christ alone.

I hope that this book helps us to combat our propensity to make success our god, and our insistence at minimizing our offence or ignoring such behavior. Even worse are feeble attempts to rationalize our idolatry by cloaking it in the spiritual language of good stewardship. A friend wrote to me of the challenge of success:

"I'm daily tempted to work for other's approval and confronted with my own inadequacies ...which I try to hide under the carpet of success..."

I think this insight was part of the solution and I wrote to a friend who was struggling through a similar journey:

"Well done! The first step is acknowledging the problem. Many of your colleagues will never come to the realization that they serve an idol of seeking the approval of others. It is an identity that will eventually kill them in this world and the next. Of those who become aware of it, many fail to see it for what it is: idolatry and sin."

We are not alone. In the Bible, the most "successful" characters (which I define loosely as those who were used mightily for God's glory) were also ones who regularly fell short...and fell into sin. Moses' successes led him to take things into his owns hands and commit murder. Jonah's success was tainted with misgivings about God's will. David's power led him to sin, and unwillingness to acknowledge that sin led to even further sin. Jacob, the father of the Jewish nation, experienced revelations from God and great success but this was mixed in with sin, manipulation and trickery. Interestingly, it was in his failure and inadequacy, and not his success, that he actually found God as he wrestled. The fact my second child is named Jacob partly reflects my identification with the struggle of Jacob. In the New Testament Peter, the rock, became one of the most successful of the disciples. However, in striving for worldly success, that is, averting Jesus' failure, he even prompts Jesus to call him Satan. Yet God graciously sent messengers, curses, wilderness experiences, and suffering to turn these people back to Himself.

Likewise, I continue to struggle with the sin of addiction to success. I continue to strive to achieve goals. This addiction is partly driven by a need to prove self-worth in worldly terms. I continue to struggle to see my identity in Him…and not what I do. However, that didn't prevent God from using the *fallible faithful* in the Bible for His glory and it does not stop him from using us. Our failings will not stop God from using us for His glory. But we need to be prompted to continually examine our hearts to identify when we stray across the line into self-seeking. At times God will send friends, like my Harvey Fellow colleagues at the summer institutes, to convict us. At other times perhaps he even sends suffering and failure to make us aware of our need for Him?

So does this mean we should just accept that this problem cannot be conquered in a fallen world and so resign ourselves to striving for success? By no means! Sanctification is an ongoing process for the rest of our lives. The awareness of our sinfulness - even the sinfulness in doing "good works" – grounds us firmly in the total sufficiency of His amazing grace. In this awareness our identity becomes firmly rooted in an acute and painful awareness of our sinful nature. The beauty of it is that this painful understanding means that even in our successes we are firmly grounded in the knowledge of grace and His love to us mere sinners. This deep awareness of my brokenness and sinfulness helps me "count all else but loss compared with the greatness of knowing Jesus, our Lord."

6. Conclusion

In conclusion, then, success in my professional academic world is not wrong, but it has been dangerous for me. Insidiously, success has time and again come to define who I am. My value has often become entwined in striving for worldly recognition: the success drug. The gift of my daughter, coming in complete weakness, has taught me more about this problem than any well-reasoned book. She has taught me that value is not in achieving at work or even in doing great things at work so that people will turn to God. In her disability she has epitomized that value is in being created in God's image, being loved by Him, and being used for His glory both in our success and more often in our failure.

God has given us gifts that this world values and we should continue to use them. However, I know I will go back and forth over a grey line of success for God's glory vis-à-vis success for my glory. May God help us, day by day, to have our identity firmly in Him so that in success or failure, we are not destroyed but strengthened! Ultimately we will only completely succeed when we ultimately fail in life! Only in death and only in complete submission to the hand of God will I fully understand these things. Only in the grace of God can I really be "successful."

In conclusion, I ask you to join me in a prayer for all our successful Christian academic colleagues and professionals. Their lot is a hard one and their hearts are so vulnerable to the counterfeit god of success. Jesus' teaching on the Lord's prayer in Matthew is in the context of Jesus teaching us to undertake righteous acts faithfully and not for our name or our ends but for His name, His will and His glory. Righteous acts could equally apply to being faithful Christians in academia and professional settings. In this light I would ask you to conclude this chapter by joining me in praying the prayer that Jesus taught us to pray (Matthew 6:10-13):

'Our Father in heaven,
hallowed be your name,
your kingdom come,
your will be done on earth as it is in heaven.
Give us today our daily bread.
Forgive our sins
Save us from the time of trial,
and deliver us from evil.
For the kingdom, the power, and the glory are yours,
now and forever.
Amen.

Investing as a Calling

Soo Chuen Tan
Discerene Value Advisors LLC
USA

1. Introduction

When this book project was first announced, I thought it would be an honor to share my professional journey (thus far) with others. Then I began putting pen down to paper, and I realized just how difficult it is to write thoughtfully about this topic. One runs the risk of coming across as preachy, inauthentic, hypocritical, or worse. When one (inevitably) experiences moral failure in the future, what one memorializes in these pages becomes particularly damning. Believing that our beliefs should be expressed by what we do, not what we say, I was also worried about "using faith as a shield." It is only thanks to the persistence of the editors that this essay got written at all.

I was privileged to receive a Harvey Fellowship to attend the Masters in Business Administration program at Harvard Business School. After graduating in 2004, I went to work as an investment analyst with a hedge fund in New York City. The next four years were a whirlwind of activity. I changed jobs and lived through a time of personal loss. Then came Lehman Brothers' bankruptcy and the near-collapse of the U.S. financial system. Several large companies with long, proud histories failed. Perpetrators of Ponzi schemes were found out. Many American households were left with debt obligations significantly larger than the value of their assets. In the aftermath, a wave of anger swept the country as tax-payers questioned why the government was bailing out, of all people, "fat-cat" bankers on Wall Street. Stories of executive excesses did not help. "Nero buys $35,000 toilet while Wall Street burned," screamed a typical headline. Finance professionals were leaving Wall Street in droves. Like others in similar positions, I had become a little disillusioned with the apparent amorality of my field. Was it possible to live a Christian life as a professional investor? The intellectual challenge of generating wealth by making good investment decisions was engaging (especially given the financial bar-gains available at the time), but was my job intrinsically "worthwhile"? After much reflection, I decided to set up my own investment firm, Discerene (from the Latin *Discernere,* "to discern"), in May 2010.

2. Articulating the Vision

What kind of firm were we setting out to build? Early on, we articulated a few core values, among which were the following:

"We will make mistakes, but we will maintain an intrinsic hu-mility and intellectual honesty so that we learn from them, and continuously work on improving the investment process.... We are committed to being transparent with our Partners, so disclosure to our Partners will be limited only by our need to protect the interests of the Fund, and of all Partners equally."

"We will build the firm as a long-term partnership with our investors, and view each relationship as being important to the DNA of the firm. Our favorite length of partnership is "forever"... In tough times, our hope is that our Partnership will "fall in," not "fall out." We are committed to finding the right Partners and building strong relationships with each in order to achieve this outcome."

"Our challenges as we grow are also cultural, not just structural. Sociologically, the bare-knuckled world of finance can be a tough world to be in, but not of. In navigating the little Discerene sailboat through the inevitable choppy waters, we believe that it is critically important to sail by a strong internal compass. This compass has to be deontic, not consequentialist, at its core: we must be able and willing to do the right thing even if this is against our best interests, and in so doing – to further mangle the metaphor – to let the chips fall where they may."

3. The *Telos* of an Investment Firm: Does Professional Investing Have Intrinsic Worth?

In his book "Business as a Calling: Work as an Examined Life,"American philosopher, author and diplomat Michael Novak lists the first three "internal responsibilities" of any business as: (1) to satisfy customers with goods and services of real value (2) to make a reasonable return on the funds entrusted to the business corporation by its investors, and (3) to create new wealth. Novak quotes Robert Goizueta, former Chairman and Chief Executive Officer of Coca-Cola:

"While we were once perceived as simply providing services, selling products, and employing people, business now shares in many of the responsibilities for our global quality of life. Successful companies will handle this heightened sense of responsibility quite naturally, if not always immediately. I say this not because successful business leaders are altruistic at heart. I can assure you, many are not. I say it because they will demand that their companies remain intensely focused on the needs of their customers and consumers."

For an investment firm, these three imperatives are one and the same. As stewards of investors' capital, the job of an investment firm is to generate good long-term returns on that capital. Novak quotes Robert Goizueta again:

"[Given that] billions of shares of publicly-held companies are owned by foundations, universities and the like, one should never forget the multiplier effect in the world of philanthropy, and the benefit to society, that each dollar increase in the value of those shares brings about. If a foundation owns, let's say, 50 million shares of Coca-Cola stock, for each dollar that our stock price increases, that foundation will be required to give out an additional $2.5 million."

For example, a large proportion of Discerene's investors are university endowments and charitable foundations, including those with missions that we think are particularly worthwhile. The firm also counts among its clients philanthropic families who have made tangible differences with their giving. We now work primarily for investors whose causes we believe in.

The next three "internal responsibilities" that Novak lists are (4) to create new jobs, (5) to defeat envy through generating upward mobility and putting empirical ground under the conviction that hard work and talent are rewarded, and (6) to promote invention and ingenuity.

At Discerene's founding, we expressed these thus: "We are committed to creating a culture that values personal integrity and character, humility and intellectual honesty, a passion for investing as a craft, honest effort and hard work toward our common goals. We have a team environment that is based on trust and mutual respect, and this will serve as the foundation for open and constructive debate. We are committed to the learning and development of every member of the firm regardless of experience, and to the recognition of excellence. We want to be a "home" to a small team of bright, thoughtful, intellectually curious, honest and humble individuals who are self-motivated and unafraid to roll up their sleeves, are willing to think critically and independently – reasoning from first principles instead of relying on conventional wisdom, who hold themselves to high personal and professional standards, and are temperamentally suited to patient, long-term investing. We want each member of the team to tap-dance to work every day, deriving fulfillment from our doing the best job we can being good stewards."

4. Market Failure or Moral Failure?

Novak's final item on the business "internal responsibility" list – (7) to diversify the interests of the republic – is perhaps the most worthy of discussion. To quote Novak: "The economic interests of some citizens are, in an important sense, at cross-purposes with the economic interests of others, and this [business activity] is crucial to preventing the tyranny of the majority."

Here, an investment firm plays a specific role, to help society allocate capital efficiently between competing potential uses of it. If investment professionals did our jobs well, capital will be directed to enterprises and ventures that are the most deserving of it. Adam Smith's "invisible hand" is really many individual actors making capital allocation decisions.

However, if the capital market "worked," why were billions of dollars directed into subprime mortgage loans that should never have been made? There is evidence that at least some industry actors believed that these did not make good business sense at the time (not merely after the fact). One problem for the industry is that mammon is a seductive master. Warren Buffett, among the world's most successful investors, described the psychology of greed:

"The line separating investment and speculation, which is never bright and clear, becomes blurred still further when most market participants have recently enjoyed triumphs. Nothing sedates rationality like large doses of effortless money. After a heady experience of that kind, normally sensible people drift into behavior akin to that of Cinderella at the ball. They know that overstaying the festivities – that is, continuing to speculate in companies that have gigantic valuations relative to the cash they are likely to generate in the future – will eventually bring on pumpkins and mice. But they nevertheless hate to miss a single minute of what is one helluva party. Therefore, the giddy participants all plan to leave just seconds before midnight. There's a problem though: They are dancing in a room in which the clocks have no hands."

A second problem for the industry is that principal-agent issues are formidable. For example, many financial professionals responsible for directing capital into subprime mortgages (through originating loans, or structuring, syndicating, and trading securities) made a lot of money from their activities. Few were asked to return the money they made from these activities.

Ultimately, it is difficult to design compensation schemes that truly align interests over appropriate time horizons. We decided that the best way for one to regulate one's own behavior is to embed it in "core values," not economics. If one commits to only acting as an honest and prudent steward of capital, one is less likely to be led astray by the siren sound of quick wealth.

5. Where the Rubber Meets the Road: Determining a "fair" Fee Structure for an Investment Firm

As we know, lofty ideals are easier to articulate than to practice. A commitment to doing the right thing is one thing. Discerning the right thing to do in a given situation is another. Executing and following through on that right course of action is yet another challenge altogether.

Economists are trained to think that the "fair" price for any good or service is what the market can bear for it. However, the market is not always efficient, especially during times of irrational exuberance. After the financial crisis, fees that investment firms charged seemed absurdly high given how poorly they preserved capital.

When Discerene was launched, we decided that we would set our fee structure not at what the market would bear, but what we thought was fair if we were on the other side of the table: i.e., what we would be willing to pay someone else to manage our money. The fees we decided to charge were significantly below prevailing market levels. We also thought it important to include claw-backs to the incentive fees we charged. For example, we would collect an incentive fee in a year in which we generated large profits for our investors. But if we lost money the next year, our investors would "claw back" some of the incentive fees previously payable to us. We thought that this would reduce the "heads I win, tails you lose" structure of traditional hedge funds, in which hedge fund managers would generate outsized fees for themselves if they made money for their investors, but only their investors would be stuck with losses if the hedge funds lost money. However, we found that potential investors began asking for fee breaks on top of the fees we were offering. The thinking went along the lines of "if they are cutting fees, they must really need business." Had we made a commercial mistake? Were investment funds in fact Giffen goods, i.e., perceived to be more desirable the higher the fees charged? We also thought twice about our conception of fairness. Could we determine what was fair, objectively speaking, given our own vested interests? Ultimately we decided that being "fair" meant (i) treating others as we would like to be treated if we were in their shoes, (ii) treating all our clients equitably, and (iii) being honest with ourselves on whether we were being true to the first two principles.

6. Identifying the Bounds of Morality in Investing

Philosopher and author Iris Murdoch wrote that "the moral life… is something that goes on continually, not something that is switched off in between the occurrence of explicit moral choices. What happens in between such choices is indeed what is crucial." However, in the investment business, moral dilemmas do have a habit of cropping up.

For example, certain profitable companies operate in morally and politically charged industries. The lines we draw at Discerene include not investing in tobacco companies, and allowing individual members of the firm decline to invest in particular companies or industries with which they are personally morally uncomfortable. Then there are the shades of grey. Some widely accepted business practices are ethically challenging. For example, pharmaceutical companies in some parts of the world pay cash "incentives" to doctors who prescribe their drugs. We find these practices objectionable, but do we then condone the (legal) practice of U.S. pharmaceuticals companies that send their favorite prescribing doctors to seminars (that just happen to be) in Hawaii or Florida? There are also "fallen" companies. For example, what are the moral implications of investing in Enron or Olympus after fraud at those companies had been discovered? We have decided that we would indeed be willing to invest in companies with such "hair" on them: we can often buy these businesses at attractive prices after fraud is uncovered, and the companies themselves (often with new teams of executives) are given the opportunity to redeem themselves and start to regain the trust of their shareholders.

We find that there are often no bright-line rules that we can apply to all fact patterns. However, this does not mean that there are no lines to be crossed. As a practical matter, one does well to listen to the "quiet, still voice" of one's conscience in daily decisions. When something does not feel right, it usually is not.

7. The Speck in a Brother's Eye

As in other fields, business professionals are sometimes asked to give references on others. I have struggled with these requests on a few occasions. Declining to provide a reference is sometimes the most damaging reference of all. Several years ago, I grappled with a difficult request, and decided to consult my spiritual director. What did he think – how should I balance the claims of justice vs. mercy? His counsel was striking: I should think about whether I can act out of Christian charity. After all, "mercy is the perfection of justice."

I looked this up. There was Micah 6:8: "He has shown you, O mortal, what is good. And what does the Lord require of you? To act justly and to love mercy and to walk humbly with your God."

Catholic author and columnist Elizabeth Foss reflects on the quality of mercy: "It's a simple thing to call a wrong a wrong. It's a simple thing to point out someone's faults or failings. We are a people who have been shown God's goodness; we are required to do more. We are called to act justly and love mercy. Remember: Every person's shortcoming causes her suffering. It is a wound. Jesus came to tenderly dress the wounds and to heal the suffering of the sinner…That's a very different concept from the one of judging, scolding, punishing and humiliating. Finally, we are called to walk humbly with our God. In our humility, we are not quick to condemn our neighbor. We recognize our own sinfulness. We recognize that we are nothing without Him and that we are limited in our own capacity to understand another person. We respond with genuine humility when we are gentle, allow ourselves to be infused with the kindness, goodness and mercy of Our Lord, and become ministers of that mercy…"

Over time, I have come to learn that one can be both honest and kind. This does not mean ignoring failings. It is sometimes necessary to "speak truth," even when this is uncomfortable. Nevertheless, one can learn to look more closely into the strengths of others, so as to speak more sincerely when called upon to describe them.

8. Walking by Faith

As the years pass, I realize more and more that living out one's faith in one's professional life requires much wisdom and discernment: it is not only about not doing certain things or living by certain precepts (though these are important as well). Even wisdom is insufficient: often we do not know, even after much reflection, what the "right thing to do" is. Being a Christian in the world also involves a daily walking by faith – which ultimately requires trust in God's love, and in the steadiness of His hand in our lives and our work. In the words of Pope Francis: "(L)et us believe the Gospel when it tells us that the kingdom of God is already present in this world and is growing, here and there, and in different ways: like the small seed which grows into a great tree (cf. Matthew 13:31-32)… Because we do not always see these seeds growing, we need an interior certainty, a conviction that God is able to act in every situation, even amid apparent setbacks: "We have this treasure in earthen vessels" (2 Corinthians 4:7). This certainty is often called "a sense of mystery." It involves knowing with certitude that all those who entrust themselves to God in love will bear good fruit (cf. John 15:5). This fruitfulness is often invisible, elusive and unquantifiable. We can know quite well that our lives will be fruitful, without claiming to know how, or where, or when… The Holy Spirit works as he wills, when he wills and where he wills; we entrust ourselves without pretending to see striking results. We know only that our commitment is necessary."

Working Knowledge: Faith, Vocation, and the Evidence of Things Unseen

Caleb D. Spencer
Department of English
Azusa Pacific University
Azusa, California

> "Faith is the substance of things hoped for,
> the evidence of things unseen" Hebrews 11:1

1. Introduction: from Balance to Knowledge

When I was first contacted about this volume, I planned to write a chapter in which I outlined the ways that my life was not particularly balanced and how this was, I hoped, a principled decision rather than a passively induced state, the eventual byproduct of circumstances I simply acquiesced to. In preparation for writing that chapter I did quite a bit of thinking about the nature of Christian vocation and the separation of private life and public work that are so common in our contemporary ways of understanding human life. I was struck while reading the Institutes, that Calvin, for one, did not think of life in neat compartments in which work was one component of the individual's life and the private life was another, and so, living at the cusp of modernity, he most likely would not have understood our need to integrate our lives, nor our need to balance our work and our private lives. If both our Christian faith and our vocation and our public and private lives were the same, no integration and no balance would have been necessary. It was these thoughts about the need to balance work and private life that I was really interested in following out.

However, midway through the writing of that chapter I had an experience that changed my mind about what I wanted the topic of this essay to be. I went as a co-host to a conference for graduate students who are trying to quite intentionally integrate their vocation and faith and I had a surprising experience. In countless conversations I came to realize that some of the younger fellows had really not given much thought to the possible models that one might have for integrating one's faith into one's vocation. Clearly all intended to integrate their faith and their public work, but they didn't appear to have considered some of the different ways others had come to articulate that integration. Thus they saw their particular understanding of what it meant to be a Christian in their field without much reference to the alternate possibilities that might be available to them and even when someone else in the same small group would speak with obviously different presuppositions about what such integration looked like, the two speakers would never really meet on the ground of their presuppositional difference.

To illustrate my point, allow me to give just one quick example. I was a part of a small group at the conference in which a group of fellows from the same field (business management) were talking about their post-grad school careers and how to be Christians in them. One was suggesting that to be a Christian in their shared field meant to interrogate (based on their Christian convictions about justice and God's desires for the world) the most basic assumptions of management and be a vocal witness (prophetic) for change in that field. Another fellow seemed to think that being a Christian in business entailed being a good witness by being an exemplary manager, inviting people to church, and displaying Christian virtue. And a third fellow suggested that being a Christian helped her know what to do in her management decisions, that it gave her better access to the truth and thereby made her a better manager. From what I saw in the conversation, none seemed to see the others as threatening their view of integrating faith and vocation, and none, from what I could tell, saw the others as making a claim upon them, a claim that demanded that they either become a prophetic witness, an evangelist in their management position, or that they tap their faith for its power to help them know what to do in business. I guess this didn't exactly surprise me (being critical of other people's ways of being a Christian isn't exactly the point of these types of conferences), but, then again, given the critical self-consciousness and plain intelligence of so many of these fellows, I was taken aback by the lack of creative possibility such a limited palate of conceptual models seemed to offer my friends. More particularly, I was surprised in that small group that there wasn't more of an argument about what constituted faithful Christian integration, as the conversation was wonderful, deep and informed on the purpose of business and its singular prerogatives, even as there seemed to be a general and pervasive pluralism about the purpose of the Christian in business.

It was conversations like these that got me thinking about my own field, English literature, and its rich history of scholars who have attempted to not only integrate their faith and their practice as scholars, but have also written and spoken about that practice. I knew from previous work that I had done on the nature of Christian literary scholarship that there was in my field, just as among these business school students, disagreement about what constituted faithful integration of faith and literary scholarship. This made me wonder about whether the more helpful chapter, rather than the "work life balance" piece, would be one that took the question of integration seriously and looked (broadly) at the models that have been forwarded for such integration. And further, that it would be worthwhile to write about the normative force of these models, looking at how they can't be equal and different, at least at the point where, like the business conversation I was a part of, they make claims upon Christians that are binding and in disagreement with one another about the best way to be a Christian in our professions. It was this normative dimension that I believed had to also be addressed in any taxonomy of integrationist models.

And at the same time, to return to the issue brought up by the third interlocutor in the conversation among the business folks, it seems to me that if we were going to think about Christians and their vocations, it would be worthwhile to consider what, if anything, Christians might uniquely contribute to their vocations as Christians. For example, is there a particular type of Christian businessman or woman (or types)? Or are there Christian doctors, not just doctors who happen to also be Christians, but doctors who are in some fundamental way different as doctors because they are Christians? I am of course aware that the whole category of vocation as career is a vexed category, but for the purposes of this paper, I am going to simply use vocation, career and profession somewhat interchangeably, not because I am unaware that the vocation of a Christian is larger than any career or profession (that vocation is described as "to glorify God and enjoy Him forever" in my tradition), but because it seems worth asking whether or not Christians pursue this part of that wider vocational purpose in any principled peculiar way. To this end, I plan to spend some time discussing the field that I know best, literary scholarship, in order to begin to get a sense for some of the possible models for Christian vocation. I hope that looking at the ways that Christians have defined Christian literary criticism will help us to think about how we might define (and not define) the Christian businesswoman or Christian doctor as well.

2. Christian Literary Criticism

In what follows, I am concerned to determine what, if anything, Christians can contribute to literary studies that non-Christian critics cannot. It is not unusual today for Christian literary scholars, like people in other fields, to assume because they are Christians the work they do is also in some sense Christian. But of course the question is in what sense? In the end, I will suggest that most of the time when doing literary critical work, Christianity makes little, if any, principled difference to this scholarly activity and, more strongly, cannot make any theoretical difference unless its participants are willing to adopt theophanic models of reading. Furthermore, and more controversially, it will follow from this that Christian faith has no principled and generalizable epistemic effect on any vocational field. Of course, just to tame any controversy from the outset, it will not be the purpose of this essay to suggest that Christian scholars (or doctors, or any other vocational subgroup) have nothing unique or valuable to offer their vocations. Only that this argument is against some of the theoretical claims made by Christians about their particular callings' "Christian-ness."

In spite of the dire predictions of secularization theorists for over a century, religion has surged to the forefront of many public conversations in the last decade, including in academe. Religion's return to the Academy is marked by conferences, special issues of journals and magazines, books, articles, and curiosity from scholars who are themselves indifferent to religion as a form of personal commitment. At the same time, religion has become of interest again in literary scholarship. And even outside the Academy it has become a platitude to comment upon the rise in church attendance after 9-11, the prominence of faith on the national political scene, and the centrality of Islam and Christianity in the global south and east. These and other signs suggest that it is quite possible to explain the return of religion to English by reference to events that have occurred outside it: English has returned to religion because the world around it has.

But there may be some more properly academic reasons for the new importance of Christianity in literary studies: the erosion of the rationalist and scientistic foundation of the academic enterprise. It is no longer clear that there are two distinct categories of knowledge: rational, scientifically verifiable beliefs (perspicuous and available to all who correctly apply their innate rational faculties and the appropriate methods) and faith-based beliefs (acculturated and requiring superstitious "leaps of faith" to be compelling). Instead many, if not most, scholars now work under the assumption that there are simply beliefs which guide the rest of a person's commitments, all of which are perspicuous to the person who holds them but which are not innate or guaranteed by the faculty of human reason.

As a result of the rejection of the first category of knowledge, many recent epistemological conceptions repudiate the long held belief that religious conviction happens in a way distinct from other kinds of complex conviction. What follows from this move towards anti-foundationalism (the epistemology most often referred to simply as "postmodern") is that the central role of conviction to the academic enterprise comes to the foreground and Christianity as well as other religions no longer seem at an epistemic disadvantage for having been based upon faith/belief.

For instance, Catholic theologian and scholar of Indian Buddhism, Paul Griffiths, in a review of Stanley Hauerwas' 2001 Gifford Lectures (subsequently published as With the Grain of the Universe), explains that "the demand [by some philosophical foundationalists/modernists] for justification (or vindication or support) of Christian conviction from any source other than itself is misplaced" (74) and this is because "Christian conviction is not epistemologically guilty until proven innocent; it is, rather, epistemologically innocent until proven guilty. And in this it is like every other complex conviction (Marxism, Buddhism, Confucianism, and so on) about the nature of human persons and the world in which we find ourselves" (74). Griffiths asserts that "it is…an ordinary feature of human conviction that those who hold particular complex convictions may defensibly continue to do so without having or being able to give independent epistemic support for them" (emphasis mine, 74). Griffiths' point is that there is nothing about religion that makes its rejection of the "epistemologists' demand" for "independent epistemic support" more difficult because there are no such things as independent foundations, that is, no grounds which are not themselves beliefs. Griffiths concludes that we are "all sectarians, which is to say that we all inhabit a form of life whose central commitments neither can nor need be validated or justified or vindicated independently of assuming them true. The only important distinction, conceptually, is between those who know this and those who do not" (75). In short, as Griffith's summary of recent epistemological debates suggests, recent theoretical turns have made religious ways of knowing identical to non-religious ways of knowing, thereby eliminating the notion that religious people need to demonstrate the truthfulness of their position by reference to an independent foundation more certain than faith. And thus the religious scholar whose work is carried on within the framework of his or her religious convictions does not begin from a position of epistemic disadvantage.

But if there are no epistemic disadvantages to being a Christian critic, might there be some epistemic advantages to being a Christian critic? Or to pose the problem as a question of literary theory, if faith-based readings are now understood by many to be the only possible kind of readings, what readings are uniquely enabled by Christian faith? And further, what can literary scholars glean from theological paradigms to enable them to do Christian literary studies, where Christian is not simply a description of the identity of the producer, but also fundamentally a modifier of the noun phrase "literary stud-ies," that is, where the scholarship as well as the scholar are uniquely Christian? It would appear that if Christianity has become interesting again, that there might be something im-portant for the Christian critic to offer. The question is what.

One might begin with the fairly common idea that Christian criticism is scholarship in which the content of the inquiry is the distinguishing Christian feature. Critics who practice this variety of criticism see it as their job to spell out the themes, metaphors, and allusions in texts—such as Dante's Divine Comedy—that are indebted to Christianity. These scholars may defend such criticism on the grounds that Christians need to guard the wealth of Christian history and texts from mar-ginalization in an academic setting often hostile to the texts of classical Christianity. And if we are to understand the great many texts created by Christians we need critics to do this.

However, we don't need Christians to do it. There is noth-ing about this kind of scholarship that requires one to be a Christian. Even if it might be empirically the case that scholars who are likely to recognize theological overtones in texts are themselves religious, there is no need for them to believe the theology, do the practices, or have lived the history, anymore than a scholar of ancient Hittite religion needs to be a practitio-ner of that religion to understand and explain the theological references in the Gilgamesh epic. One can be a Christian and be theologically and historically aware of Christianity, just as one can be a non-believer and be theologically and histori-cally aware of Christianity. Neither Stanley Fish nor Jeffrey Knapp, for instance, is a self-professed Christian and yet both Fish's works on Milton and Knapp's work on Shakespeare and

Christianity display an erudite capacity to deal subtly with the nuances of the Christian religion. Even without such examples, it is possible to say, on the basis of the genetic fallacy alone, that this type of scholarship, while valuable and necessary, doesn't require Christians for its existence.

Another common type of "Christian" scholarship is that which sees literature as primarily a prompt for theological reflection. Because literature depicts a kind of (often latent) theology, it offers a complicated exemplification of the human situation and an alternative theology to the rarified discourse of academic theology, similar to what Martha Nussbaum thinks literature offers philosophy. Just as, for example, the theorist of gender sees both exemplification of gender oppression in literary texts and also primary construction of that oppression, practitioners of this type of scholarship see literature as both exemplifying and producing a primary theology. But again, one needn't be a Christian in order to do theological reflection, any more than one would need to be a person of an oppressed gender to recognize gender oppression and construction in a text. Beliefs are not required, only knowledge.

A third type of Christian criticism is more complicated because it does indeed seem to require Christian conviction. These critics are perhaps best described as integrationists in that they see the Christian faith as being integral to the practice of their criticism. T.S. Eliot's conception of the normative power of Christian views of truth, of reality, and of culture provides the model for applying Christianity's basic Weltanschaaung as the ground for evaluative criticism. The logic is to determine what Christianity holds to be true, beautiful or good; then determine what the work in question deems true, beautiful or good; then compare and contrast; and conclude by determining if the work is of value on the basis of the relationship between the two. Thus Leland Ryken writes: "To ignore God and spiritual values as secular art does is a monstrosity in God's world. No matter how great an artist's technique might be, or how sensitive the portrayal of human experience is, a work of art is finally false if it limits reality to the temporal, physical world, or omits God's existence from its picture of reality" (221). Good art in this formulation is that which is true, and since secular art is based upon the exclusion of God—a falsehood—it cannot be true and is therefore not good.

This type of criticism, however, does not require Christian convictions; it requires only that the critic know what the criteria are. Christian belief can inform the practice of evaluative criticism, but a non-Christian critic could just as easily extrapolate the criticism that a Christian would have expressed. Yet even though knowing the judgment would not require one to be a Christian, actually occupying the judgment—having the conviction that this artwork is better than this other one on the basis of Christian commitment—does require one to be a Christian. A critic need not be a Christian to know the judgment, but he or she does have to be a Christian to believe it. In this case, deploying a Christian aesthetic would actually require Christian faith.

The fourth species of Christian scholarship is perhaps the most contested and, to my mind, the most interesting. It is practiced by scholars who claim that Christianity makes a theoretical difference to their reading because it shapes, forms or constructs the texts that they engage. Where the first three types all made claims on the basis of knowledge, this last type of scholarship claims that Christian identity shapes the identity of outside objects. In other words, these scholars claim that without the "Christian" before "scholar" they wouldn't be able to see or do what they are seeing or doing because what they see and what they do are functions of what they are.

Many such scholars follow the "interpretive community" model of idealism, arguing that Christians construct different texts when they read because of their Christianity. These scholars have been persuaded that we only know by mediated perception. They follow the Stanley Fish of Is There a Text in this Class? who argued that interpretive communities and their strategies of reading "exist prior to the act of reading and therefore determine the shape of what is read rather than, as is usually assumed, the other way around" (171). In the case of the Christian critic, Christianity functions as the interpretive community so that by being a Christian the reader constructs (writes) texts rather than reconstructing them—hence the constructive "idealism." Often these critics, as Fish himself did at times, conclude that because all of our knowledge comes to us through the mediation of interpretive community it is all equally good, just different. Thus the Jew who "reads" Genesis with Jewish convictions about reality is acting in a way consistent with his interpretive community and his reading is therefore just as valid as the Christian who sees in Adam a type of Christ. However to conclude that all readings are equal but different is incoherent because such a conclusion is itself a universal claim and therefore stands outside the assumption of universal mediation that these scholars presume. To be a Christian, however, cannot ever be to think that the Christian account of reality—or a particular text—is simply the Christian community's account, because that account itself makes claims about the world that are either true or false for everyone. While Fish's interpretive community model is a powerful account (as Fish now acknowledges) of the sociology of interpretation, it does not produce a compelling account of the nature of Christian criticism.

Another subset of critics who believe that Christianity provides a unique epistemology or methodology, argue that their beliefs enable them to see things in texts that others cannot see; they may argue, for instance, that to be a Christian is to be more humble or charitable and this in turn becomes a model for Christian interpretation and scholarly practice. Two problems intrude: such theories fail in principle unless critics are willing to deny virtues—caritas for example in Alan Jacobs' The Hermeneutics of Love—to non-Christians. Secondly, even if it is empirically the case that Christians value charity and this often leads to better criticism, it does not follow that Christian identity provides Christian critics with a literary theory that allows them to do better or more faithful critical work.

The third subset of critics who believe that Christianity provides a unique epistemology consist of those critics and theologians who argue that literary texts, like other art forms, can be revelatory and that the role of the Christian critic is to mediate that revelation to those who don't have the eyes to see it. This revelatory, prophetic mode is the most contentious and the most counter-cultural, and what is more, this kind of reading really does seem to be available only to the Christian scholar. If Christian scholars want to test the post-secularity of the present academic world, I suggest they do so by attempting to re-sacralize literary experience not only by articulating theories of theophany but by producing readings in which theophanic experiences are described. Such readings would imitate the mode of artifactual engagement demonstrated by Paul Tillich's discussions of modern visual art and Nathan Scott's analyses of modern literary texts. They would suggest the revelation and presence of the divine as manifested through the extra-intentional effects of a work, or to paraphrase Tillich "if the idea of God as the power of being includes all of reality, then everything that artistically expresses reality (i.e., every artistic form) will express God, whether it intends to do so or not" (Palmer 144).

Few readers will have a problem when scholars say, "The Christian faith of this author caused him to write in such and such a way" or "My knowledge of Christian theology enables me to understand this image as alluding to Christ's passion," but writing "What the poem reveals, in addition to the poet's intention, is the truth of God's commandment that we love our neighbor" or "For the reader, the story mediates God's own presence" might raise a few eyebrows. In another context it might be both useful and pleasurable to delineate the reasons that the latter two would be contested in our present world, but here it should suffice to say that the dogmatism of the first and the divine self-expression implied by the second would be heavily contended in the present Academy, as much among scholars who are themselves religious as by those who are not.

To conclude this section and return to the broader questions about vocation and faith, let me be clear that my point is not to recommend a single model for Christian scholars, but like Stanley Hauerwas I am inclined to think that Christianity by definition will always be marginal and that the desire to make it normal (or universal) will always result in dissolution of the unique message of the Gospel. If we are to contribute as scholars to the present discourse about religion, I think that we must do so with a clear understanding of what we alone are capable of offering. Theophanic experience may be the only thing that we can offer in a world no longer hostile to the structure of our belief, but still deeply hostile to its content. And yet, perhaps even theophanic practices of reading cannot be limited to Christian believers. For, if the testimony of Scripture is to be trusted, it seems that God has chosen to reveal Himself at various times to those who, prior to that revelation, didn't know Him or didn't know Him properly—think here of Abram, Saul of Tarsus, and the Magi. In other words, theophanic modes of reading may not even require the regenerative work of the Holy Spirit to have started and so it may be argued then that even theophanic reading is not fundamentally a Christian critical practice. And if this is the case, then it may be that Christian identity has no fundamental effect upon the practice of criticism and that the notion of Christian criticism is simply a mistake.

3. From Literary Criticism to Vocation

But if Christian criticism is potentially a problem if we are not to invoke the Holy Spirit's work, does it follow that the integration of Christianity and vocation is potentially a problem too? In other words if there are potential problems for Christian criticism if one is not willing to make deeper epistemic claims about the nature of Christian knowing, does it follow that there are the same kinds of problems for Christians and vocation? After all, many vocations are more centrally about doing than they are about knowing, and as such the analogy between a type of work that requires one to know something and a type of work that requires one to do something seems potentially compromised. Is there really much that non-literary critics can learn from this delineation of different kinds of literary scholarship?

First, it seems clear, but worth mentioning, that the types of literary scholarship I described above have corollaries in many, if not all, other fields. For example, there are many people outside of literary scholarship, academe, and even the broader fields of "knowledge work," who think that the substance of their integration of faith and vocation lies in the "content" of their work, just like the literary scholars who focus on Christian literature. So for example, many in policy development and NGO work see that work as being focused upon the equitable distribution of scarce resources (medical expertise, city planning, etc.) that follows directly from Christian sources. The critique of the uniqueness of this work would be the same as the critique of the literary scholars: Christian faith is not necessary for this work even if it is sometimes a contributing cause.

Similarly, the third type of literary scholarship, aesthetic judgment from a Christian perspective, seems to have many corollaries in other fields. For example, Christians in politics might see themselves as judging public choices from within a Christian framework just as the literary scholar judges the work from within a Christian aesthetic framework. Just as with the Christian aesthetic judgment, to know what the Christian politician should believe and do we don't need Christians in politics, but to have anyone actually believe and do it, we do need Christians in these positions. The Christian in politics, leadership, public policy, etc. has an opportunity to try to systematically apply the Christian account of the true, the good and the beautiful in a way with public and personal consequences, surely a real form of integrating faith and vocation.

And it's finally to the fourth type of Christian scholarship that I will turn to conclude these remarks, the type that claims something epistemic for Christian faith. I would suggest that the most interesting thing that can be generalized from my discussion of Christian literary scholarship is the difficulty of thinking that Christian faith gives one privileged access to knowledge. What is true of Christian literary criticism is true of any kind of Christian understanding of integrating faith and vocation that sees the integration of faith and vocation as being about a special kind of knowledge. There are no epistemic advantages to being a Christian except those offered by the Holy Spirit, but these advantages are precisely not generalizable into a theory of Christian vocation—except of course to say that the Holy Spirit does in fact inspire people (which is hardly a workable theory of any vocation). Thus unless Christian lawyers are ready to claim that the presence of the Holy Spirit within them is what causes their particular interpretation of the law, I think that it is clear that what makes them Christian lawyers is not their special interpretation of the law, just as Christian clinicians in diagnosing a disease are not made Christian doctors by the special work of the Holy Spirit to help them make that diagnosis any more than the Christian engineers construct their bridge with the Holy Spirit's assistance. This is of course in no way to deny that the Holy Spirit has inspired interpretations of law, or that doctors have been guided by the Spirit in their work. Faith may of course aid knowledge and the Holy Spirit may inspire professionals, but that doesn't mean that this should be our theory of Christian vocation or that because the Spirit may inspire, that the Spirit will. (The question of the Holy Spirit's inspiration of the Christian artists poses an interesting, but here unanswered question about Christian vocation, since from at least Wordsworth and Coleridge people have been asking about and connecting the Spirit and the production of art. Furthermore, what is true of artists would be true more generally for any field that is more positive than analytic; in other words, fields where people make rather than make in a dependent relationship to what has already been made.)

However, my skepticism about the epistemic effect of Christian faith does not entail a general skepticism about the possibility of integrating faith and vocation. Rather I'm simply suggesting that the way of doing this generally will not be by invoking a kind of privileged knowledge for the Christian. As the rest of this volume attests there are many ways of being a Christian in one's vocation, but I want to suggest that there are a number of ways that people have thought they were being Christians in their work that are hardly unique, and in the area of accessing truth this is a particularly pernicious problem. The solution is not to deny that we know things, or even that at times the Holy Spirit has revealed things to individuals, but rather to understand that when the Spirit does his revelatory work, it is a peculiar moment of grace for which we should give thanks, but out of which we shouldn't theorize an account of our collective responsibility as Christians. In the end then, even if we aren't Christian scholars (doctors, policy makers, etc.) by what we are only able to know, we are nonetheless Christians all the same and this means that in a very serious (and beautiful) way we are the hands and feet of Christ, the working out of the Spirit's will in the world. In this we work every moment toward the redemption and restoration of God's world and to the fulfillment of Christ's Kingdom. To this truth I can only humbly proclaim: Soli Deo Gloria. Amen and Amen.

Acknowledgements

I am grateful to Susan Felch for first encouraging me to write about Christian literary scholarship, to Paul Contino and Christianity and Literature for permission to reprint material from my 2009 article "What Counts as Christian Criticism?" and to Walter Benn Michaels, Tiffany Kriner and Brian Sheerin for the helpful comments each gave me on earlier drafts of this chapter.

Works Cited

Fish, Stanley. How Milton Works. Cambridge: Harvard UP, 2001

-----. Surprised by Sin. Cambridge: Harvard UP, 1967.

-----. "Theory's Hope." Critical Inquiry 30.2 (2004): 374-78.

Griffiths, Paul J. "Witness and Conviction in With the Grain of the Universe." Modern Theology 19.1 (2003): 67-75.

Jacobs, Alan. A Theology of Reading: The Hermeneutics of Love. Boulder: Westview, 2001.

Lundin, Roger. The Culture of Interpretation: Christian Faith in the Postmodern World. Grand Rapids: Eerdmans, 1993.

-----. From Nature to Experience

-----. Emily Dickinson and the Art of Belief

------. There Before Us: Religion, Literature and Culture from Emerson to Wendell Berry

Palmer, Michael. Paul Tillich's Philosophy of Art. Berlin: Walter De Gruyter, 1984.

Royce, Josiah. The Problem of Christianity. Chicago: U of Chicago P, 1968.

Ryken, Leland. The Liberated Imagination: Thinking Christianly About the Arts. Wheaton: Harold Shaw, 1989.

Scott, Nathan A. Modern Literature and the Religious Frontier. New York: Harper & Row, 1958.

-----. The Broken Center: Studies in the Theological Horizons of Modern Literature. New Haven: Yale UP, 1966.

Tillich, Paul. On Art and Architecture. Ed John and Jane Dillenberger. New York: Crossroad, 1987.

Interruptions are not Distractions: Lessons from Teaching in Faith-steeped Conflict Zones of Southeast Asia

Laura S. Meitzner Yoder
Program in Human Needs and Global Resources
Wheaton College
Illinois, USA

1. Introduction

The contributions to this book share a distinctive posture of attentiveness to how faith is represented, expressed, and lived in public and in academic settings: how it is already present, and how our own faith in practice becomes part of our contexts. My work as professor and practitioner in environmental anthropology has taken me to places with great diversity in religious adherence and a wide range of socio-political situations that foster or circumscribe faith expression. Experiences and relationships in these places have strongly influenced how I have progressively discovered, enacted, and exercised my vocation up to this point in my life.

An enduring contribution of my involvement with the Harvey Fellows program for Christian graduate students has been the recurrent challenge to query, "How does my work today fit into the larger picture of bringing forth the kingdom of God in this time and place, with these people, in this context?" In reflecting on this question, I identify three lessons learned through my work to date: the importance of interruptibility, being alert for new models of faith expression within academia and the public sphere, and patience in building professional relationships. I conclude with comments on specific policy opportunities for expatriate Christian academics.

I draw the lessons here from seven years in three locations around the Indonesian archipelago: Papua, Timor, and Aceh. Although each region has a unique religious and political context, they share several commonalities: strong and thoroughgoing expression of faith in the public arena; recent, widespread trauma from civil conflict; and being considered an undesirable post among regional professionals because of challenging physical conditions and political instability. My first faculty placement in Southeast Asia was in as marginal and peripheral a setting as could be imagined, on nearly every front: a branch campus of the state university on the difficult-to-access island of New Guinea in strongly Protestant West Papua, Indonesia. I was assigned to the Community Service Unit of the Agriculture & Forestry Faculty, teaching and overseeing field programs with indigenous villagers in the interior. (One reason given to me for an expatriate faculty placement in this position was the difficulty of finding local academics willing to take on the task of working there!) This was a region with an active separatist movement and central government military response, extreme difficulties in transportation, and the basic living conditions inherent to life in a remote rainforest region.

Following this experience, as a Harvey Fellow I conducted my dissertation research and subsequent work in a rural enclave district of majority Catholic East Timor, then newly independent from Indonesia and recovering from the social effects and physical destruction of protracted conflict. Then immediately upon completion of my Ph.D. (Social Ecology/Forestry & Environmental Studies, Yale University), I spent three years as one of a few Christian faculty at the large public university in Banda Aceh, Indonesia. This region was rebuilding from the massive December 2004 earthquake and tsunami, which killed 111 professors and 72 administrators at this university. Aceh was simultaneously recovering from decades of civil conflict with the central government, during which the university's rector was assassinated and the population lived in a situation of chronic stress and insecurity. The province was newly implementing Islamic syari'ah law, and it was a time of dynamic social and political change. I initially taught a wide range of science classes which were lacking professors, and eventually also headed a collaborative initiative through the University of Melbourne, Australia to train and to mentor hundreds of local civil servants, faculty, and non-governmental organization staff from the whole span of disciplines in social science research methods, to contribute to the reconstruction process of the region.

What does being a Christian academic expatriate look like in these contexts? And what lessons about integrating faith and vocation are relevant to aspiring academics in the U.S.?

2. The Ministry of Interruptibility

In all three locations, populations had experienced significant trauma due to political marginalization, long-term armed conflict, and major disaster events. The people among whom I lived, researched, and taught were dealing with major deviations from their ideal life plans. In the interruptions of successive war, famine, displacement, and natural disasters, they had lost family members, suffered from severely limited opportunities and options, and endured harsh physical conditions. Living among people who were coping with loss and survival on a fundamental level put my specific professional ambitions in perspective, and kept any tendency to put faith in my own long-term dreams or plans in check. Reminded of the effects of disaster on a daily basis, I internalized others' acute awareness that our lives and fates are not within our own ambit of control, and that careers and academic trajectories are not what compose our selves in any sense of completeness. Living with disaster and loss brought into sharp relief that there is much more to life than work.

Coming from extremely well-resourced educational settings in my home universities, my new classrooms were without electricity or sufficient seating; I carried my own chalk to each class. Coping with the effects of trauma shaped and dominated the students' educational experiences. No matter what assignment I gave, undergraduate student reports referenced their lived experience of the civil conflict. For example, the tasks to interview villagers about the effects of post-tsunami salinity on their crops or to list the productive tree species in a region yielded accounts of how villagers' lives and livelihoods were affected by the conflict; ditches could not be cleared or orchards were abandoned for decades because of the political riskiness of being in those places. My agenda to cover the textbook curriculum suggested to me was frustrated; students were unable to focus on abstract lecture material that bore little relevance to their present situation.

My teaching and my relationships improved as my co-lecturers and I increasingly took local circumstances into account, based our studies on local examples, and fully employed elicitive, question-based teaching methods. This further built my appreciation for the posture of interruptibility, here within the curriculum: a willingness to look beyond our own preconceived, content-oriented goals in order to improve the educational outcomes, and personal healing opportunities, among our students. While these circumstances may seem more extreme than those typically found in a North American university classroom, faculty everywhere can be attentive and alert to the potential range of background experiences that students and colleagues are invisibly carrying into their educational settings. Compassion and listening are central to an educator's work, and this commitment drives our pedagogy to engage the specific contexts in which we teach.

Jonathan Bonk (2010:12) calls us to embrace what he terms a "missiology of interruptions": "A careful reading of the four gospels tells us mostly about pesky interruptions. With a mandate to save the world, Jesus seems to be constantly dragged into the petty but time-consuming, schedule-interrupting agendas of persons from the lowest strata of society: blind beggars, cripples, sick children, anxious parents, diseased lepers, the psychologically deranged, and so on." We read that Jesus was not so focused on getting Something Big done that He consistently ignored individual people's circumstances; we see that He chose to spend much time dealing with the very situations that those around Him interpreted as unworthy distractions, demonstrating that interacting with those very people and matters was indeed at the core of his mission. What differentiates God-given interruptions from distractions is whether they contribute to or detract from our overall purpose. Interruptibility frees me to be accessible and to relate to specific people in the path of my day, not hoarding my attention and energy for building only those linkages I may have defined as professionally strategic. How willing am I to view this interrupting situation as potentially more important work than what I had scheduled and planned for this hour, this day, or this season of life? On a broader scale, how willing am I to set aside my predetermined professional aspirations to be with people who have experienced tremendous interruption to every aspect of their lives?

Many newly graduated colleagues have commented on the shock of deceleration upon completing an intensive graduate school experience, as life takes on a more normal pace than the frenetic final months completing a dissertation or studying for the bar exam. Teaching provides ample opportunities to divert time and attention from other professional plans (of research, of writing, etc.). Even the rare new graduate who begins a prestigious tenure-track job will encounter radical change from the focused intensity of graduate school to a more varied schedule including committee meetings, advising sessions, student correspondence, and presence at school and civic events. Allowing time to meet with students and colleagues at critical decision points or in their rejoicing and mourning are central, if sometimes unanticipated parts of the task. Bonk (2010:11) remind us: "Truly Christian mission is never ethereal or speculative. It is always incarnational, addressing real human beings at the point of their personal circumstances, whatever the larger context over which neither we nor they have any control."

I have learned much about patience, grace, persistence, and joy from people whose lives have been repeatedly interrupted by situations clearly beyond their control. In situations of conflict and natural disaster, where the reality of early, unexpected death is tangible, people are so openly grateful to be alive that it seems easier to keep other problems in perspective. How tightly do we hold to our own professional ambitions? Are we open enough to recognize when God's leading may show us that "marginal" contexts are central in God's kingdom? Humbly holding our own ambitions and preconceived career goals more loosely allows us to be awed that God's sovereignty is over all the earth, while simultaneously guiding our lives.

3. Expressing Faith in the University

In Southeast Asia, faith is ubiquitous in the public sphere. It is largely accepted and expected that religion pervade every aspect of life, including university activities. Even after growing used to the everyday expressions of actively celebrated sacred holidays, course scheduling around seasonal events and scheduled space for daily religious practice in state universities, I was initially surprised that most of the research projects I supervised referred to some aspect of faith expression in the public arena or within the practice of the researcher's discipline. A biologist wrote about the vegetation change effects of formerly migratory peoples' settlement around church buildings as they came to Christian faith; an architect examined aspects of post-tsunami housing reconstruction projects for their consistency with Islamic norms on gender separation, hygiene, and prayer spaces; a physician researched sources of sexual health knowledge among youth in religious boarding schools. My students shared a generalized assumption that all subjects naturally and necessarily incorporated a religious component; I did not need to remind students to consider this aspect in their socio-cultural research proposals, as they did not exclude it in the first place. I noted how easily many students expressed their own faith-based motivations for their studies and professional aspirations. In the Christian settings, faculty and other professionals often mentioned biblical events or church practices in their presentations. With the progressive definition and implementation of syari'ah in Aceh, people constantly discussed Islamic faith and its expressions in morality, emerging law, and policy in public and private settings.

This contrast to my own university experience brought into relief the normalized, thoroughgoing secularity of the U.S. academic context I had left. Even with my long-term interests in intersections of faith and vocation, I found myself less fluent, or less practiced, in talking about these matters than my students, who had not lived in the U.S. context that largely excised matters of faith in academic settings. Building skills and confidence in communicating about faith was a major growth area for me while working in Asia. Knowing me to be a Christian, intensely curious students asked about Christian faith expressions in my home area. Because of the ubiquity of faith practice in their own experience, they had no expectation that I spoke with professional expertise in theology, but simply as one ordinary person of faith talking with another. In Aceh, several colleagues mentioned that I was the first non-Muslim they had known, and many took advantage of the first-hand opportunity to query aspects of Christianity about which they had heard. Throughout the archipelago, "humanity" is (socially, and politically) defined as or equated with having faith in God, and even middle-aged adult professionals often asked me whether it was true that in the U.S. there were people who claimed no faith whatsoever—not concealing their wonderment at how that could be possible, while still being human.

Discussions about students' views of God's work in the world were a common point of connection with students both inside and outside the classroom. In Papua and Timor, colleagues commonly mentioned Christianity's radical transformation of their societies in conversation; in Aceh, students made frequent reference to God's part in the tsunami and appropriate individual and societal responses to such an event. Students of various faith backgrounds often asked me to pray with them about family illnesses or personal crises. These interactions were also opportunities to learn about what mattered to the people around me, to understand the points at which they sought to connect with God, and to be able to better answer their questions in terms that would make sense to them.

Can you imagine teaching in faith-steeped public universities? Would this change the bounds of what you research, or how you talk about your work? What are good settings to listen and learn what matters of faith are important to the people around you at the university? How might you articulate the faith-related aspects of your own professional testimony in ways that connect to their experiences?

4. Patience and Respect in Building Relationships in Low-trust Contexts

One common feature of post-conflict situations and academia is that both tend to be (initially) low-trust settings. In civil conflict zones, people often have tightly defined circles of trusted people, often along family lines, developed out of necessity where informants abound and risks to dissenters are high. Newcomers are kept at a distance, usually for months or even years, until group members are confident that they will not betray or compromise the group. Academic settings can have similarly circumscribed zones of trust among those who understand or agree with each other, often along disciplinary lines, and newcomers are expected to prove themselves early in order to attain full inclusion.

It takes time and significant personal investment to become part of any new group, whether a new cultural context or a new academic institution. Building trust and solid relationships should be a top and early priority for a new person. In the multi-year academic assignments discussed here, I found that significant growth in my professional and personal relationships began at the end of the first year. It was only in the second year that my local colleagues openly discussed with me how closely they paid attention to my everyday behavior to gauge what sort of person I was. I was usually surprised to learn what it was that they considered notable in my life, which was usually more in the personal than the professional realm: harmony in family relationships, good connections with neighbors, and appropriate attendance at the important events in other people's lives. When people have included me in one of their circles of trust and relationship at a deeper level, they almost always have made reference to some personal action of mine that unwittingly demonstrated sufficient respect to merit inclusion.

When we are in places where people around us may have an initial inclination to distrust us—as foreigners, as Christian professionals in avowedly secular settings, as members of a minority group—the importance of being above reproach in every area of life becomes critical. For newcomers, this includes deliberately learning the local context well enough to know what shows appropriate respect and reflects morality, and what might cause offense in that setting. This provides ample opportunities to embrace humility and to practice asking forgiveness: one Indonesian colleague came to me on the annual Islamic holiday around which people ask and give forgiveness of each other, and said she was waiting for my apology in order to make things right again between us. I was at a loss; what had I done? Ten months before, I had apparently brushed by her desk chair in our close office quarters and touched her head, in a context where that action conveyed belittlement and lack of respect. Acknowledging the wrong I had committed (rather than defending it) did indeed bring about an immediate deepening in our relationship. We had many future discussions about how to deal with wrongs we have committed, from faith-based and from cultural perspectives.

5. Policy and the Expatriate Christian Academic

Working overseas affords different options than being in one's own country. Your host institution or colleagues may not know quite how to include you in the life of the university, and this can feel quite lonely at times. You cannot vote, your visa depends on passing the scrutiny of multiple security screens that exclude political activity, and you are not eligible for normal professor status where faculty are classified as civil servants in the national system. The delicate dance that expatriate academics usually perform in such a context, balancing acceptability with host institutions with a unique opportunity to address locally important issues, has provided both opportunities and constraints to the policy impact of my work.

My work has so far taken me to remote conflict zones in Southeast Asia, working with universities in regions with little name recognition. Throughout this time, the encouragement and perspective consistently emphasized by the Harvey Fellows program has challenged me to consider what unique policy intersections are indeed available to an expatriate faculty member in these "margins." Being in these places has made me less concerned with my institutional affiliation than with how attentive I am to representing Christ within my daily work, and making Him known in the connections formed through professional, church, and personal circles. These experiences have challenged my internal geographies of power, and pushed me to be alert for the forms and God-given opportunities for influence that do exist in the settings described here.

No matter where I have been, no matter how remote or peripheral to global events, that place is the center of the universe to the people who live there. This has provided a useful counterbalance to my tacit sense of what constituted the world's power centers. Residents in each of these three disparate regions have oft-cited, intricate tales detailing how their place and their people were instrumental in the formation of the world. We may take these as anthropological curiosities, or we may embrace these stories as reminders that God does not value a university graduate above an illiterate farmer. If the whole earth belongs to God, the land of a mountaintop community in East Timor is as precious as Manhattan. As the three areas where I have worked also happen to be sites of separatist movements and associated civil conflict, the local residents also have extraordinary confidence in the power of people of low status, giving me insight into some of the social inversions Jesus mentions as characteristic of God's Kingdom in new ways.

Each of these contexts had highly polarized politics related to their independence movements, and contentious local party politics. I sought God's leading and wisdom in how to proceed in this setting. As an outsider to local politics, I was able to build working relationships with members of opposing factions; this required patience, wisdom with a peacemaker's diplomacy, scrupulous adherence to ethical codes of social field research, and the creativity of an Esther. My work could not flourish without making connections on multiple fronts, so I made every effort to structure my programs to be open and courteous with members of all sides. In this respect, having the relatively neutral and equalizing institutional base of a public university was tremendously helpful, as the campus and classroom were places where people from different perspectives could meet and learn together. Serving in these universities provided many opportunities to make non-partisan contributions to the critical contemporary issues facing the society. Additionally, being a representative of the local university when I travelled throughout the region provided a high measure of legitimacy and acceptance from both government officials and local citizens; this allowed unusual access in travel-restricted areas under special military status, where people representing external organizations may not be permitted. Being grounded in local public universities provided opportunities to work directly alongside national decision-makers on a wide range of issues in ways that seem rare for academics in my home context.

Finally, being an expatriate provided unusual opportunities to be a bridge, to encourage the hearing of local and minority voices. The places and people where I worked were often considered by central authorities to be marginal by virtue of geography, ethnicity, religious minority, or questionable political allegiance. Local people saw my research as advocacy on the side of justice and of peace—not always related to the content of my research, but the very fact that I was conducting research on their own contexts, which they knew and experienced to be marginal to the interests of the central authorities. In our access to local political leaders, expatriate professors have the opportunity to faithfully represent in professional work the interests of the people among whom we work. Similarly, in valuing and stewarding the gifts of relationships that God provides in our host academic institutions, we are well situated to contribute to building and supporting a broader academic community. Where our teaching and research are oriented toward and inclusive of the justice concerns which are central to God's character, our students' and faculty colleagues' research can continue to ground state university programs in local realities and circumstances, and to inform policy in an ongoing manner.

References

Bonk, Jonathan. 2010. Thinking Small: Toward a Missiology of Interruptions. McLure Lectures, Pittsburgh Theological Seminary, September 27-28, 2010.

http://www.pts.edu/UserFiles/File/PDFs/McClure%203%20 Thinking%20Small.pdf

Sacrificial Listening: Christians, Muslims, and the Secular University

David R. Vishanoff
University of Oklahoma
U.S.A.

1. Introduction

This is the story of an ivory-tower scholar's quest for a radically Christian metaphor to govern his relationships with the Muslims he studies, his secular academic colleagues, and his students. Starting from the Parable of the Good Samaritan, I articulate a theory of sacrificial listening, and point out some of its implications for scholarship, teaching, cross-cultural and interreligious understanding, critical theory, hermeneutics, objectivity, identity, transparency, and suffering. Interwoven with this conceptual exploration is my personal story of growing faith, reckless commitment, frequent failure, and great reward.

2. Discovering Secular Colleagues

When I decided to pursue graduate study in non-Christian religions, one member of my suburban evangelical church challenged me: "Listen, David, bank tellers don't train by studying counterfeit money; they handle real bills until they can detect a false one without even looking at it." How could I explain to this concerned Christian brother that I was not studying Islam for the purpose of detecting falsehood? My goal was to understand Muslim people—not so that I could communicate the words of the Gospel more persuasively, but so that I could know and love Muslims as my neighbors and "as myself."

It was the scarcity of such a listening spirit in my parents' missionary circles, and in the Christian high school and college I attended, that prompted me to set aside mathematics and philosophy and dedicate my career to religious studies. In order to get started, I had to propose a course of independent study, because my evangelical Christian college—one of the most highly regarded in the United States—only offered courses on Christianity. How, I puzzled, could a Christian liberal arts education be complete without some attempt to understand one's religious neighbors? Mainline Christian schools taught world religions as a matter of course, but in my evangelical world non-Christian religions were taught almost exclusively as a part of missiology. That was in the late 1980s. Since September 11, 2001, American Christians have come to take for granted that of course, by all means, we must try to understand Muslims; yet to this day I know of no evangelical institution where the study of Islam can be pursued for its own

SACRIFICIAL LISTENING: CHRISTIANS, MUSLIMS, AND THE SECULAR UNIVERSITY ❧

sake, with the depth and sustained attention that are possible in the secular academy.

I enrolled, therefore, in the University of Colorado at Boulder, which was regarded in my church as a hotbed of secular liberalism—"the Berkeley of the Rockies." There I discovered the importance of loving and understanding my secular as well as my religious neighbors. Seven years in private Christian schools had left me with a vague premonition that out there, in the secular world, I would be up against "them." They would mock my faith, or attempt to corrupt it, and the best I could do would be to stand firm and hope, by dint of argument or charm, to win some over to my side. Mockery I certainly found—of my faith, but not of my person. Although my commitments were known to my professors and fellow students, I frequently had the surreal experience of listening to them chatter derisively about Christians as though their words had not the slightest bearing on anyone in the room. In their minds, Christians were caricatures of absurdity, whereas I was a colleague. They appeared not to notice the incongruity. Perhaps they never will, for the caricature itself has already begun to dissipate in many academic circles, as faithful Christians of all stripes become more and more common and identifiable in the secular academy.

To my surprise, not only did my secular neighbors accept me as an equal, I too began to identify myself with them. The questions that they asked were ones that troubled me also—especially the question of whether the cross-cultural understanding to which I aspired was actually possible. Class after class and reading after reading called into question the possibility of standing in someone else's shoes and seeing the world from someone else's perspective. Postmodern philosophers and critical theorists gradually convinced me that my goal of understanding Muslims on their own terms was chimerical and even nonsensical, because my understanding is always constructed from my particular vantage point and shaped by my own motivations and agendas. Some Christians have felt that this basic insight into the constructed nature of all human knowledge undermines the absolute truth of Christian doctrines, but I found that it only deepened my Christian convictions about the depravity of human nature and the grievous effects of the fall upon the way we learn and know. The realization that knowledge of others distorts them in ways that serve the interests of the knower was not the beginning of a postmodern slide into relativism; it was my secular colleagues' recognition of a grievous biblical truth that I had not sufficiently appreciated before.

This affinity between postmodern criticism and Augustinian anthropology is not always readily acknowledged. Even some of the more philosophically inclined members of my church still discount anything bearing the stigma of postmodernism. Most secular academics are likewise loath to countenance the possibility that Christian theology might be a useful resource for critical theory. Yet our shared concern with the self-serving nature of human knowledge presents an opportunity for Christians to serve our secular colleagues by wrestling alongside them with one of their most vexing methodological problems. Some of those colleagues do not believe they need our help, and are quite content to unmask the power dynamics of Christian and colonial discourses without ever turning the lens of critical theory upon themselves. Others, however, realize how self-serving critical theory itself can become, and of those, a few might be willing to recognize that this failure can be addressed only by a self-emptying and sacrificial kind of love that is beyond the capacity of fallen human nature. We cannot help our colleagues to realize that truth, however, unless we first acknowledge their insights into human nature, and then find ways to articulate Christian teachings using their conceptual vocabulary.

The surprise of finding myself intellectually at home among non-Christian colleagues altered my vocational aspirations. My intent had always been to return to a Christian college after doing my time, and earning my stripes, in the secular academy. My aim was to convince Christians—college students, missionaries, and the Church at large—to face their neighbors in the same confident but other-focused and attentive listening posture that Jesus took toward each person he met. I was beginning to discover, however, that the neighbors I wished to love were not just Muslims; some of them were secular intellectuals, and I seemed to have as much to learn from them as I had to offer. As I looked ahead past the Ph.D., therefore, I reset my course to become a long-term collaborator in the secular academy's discourses about Islam and about the nature of human understanding.

Before my wife, Beth, and I left Colorado, our first child, Rachel, was born—a difficult and deeply moving experience that kept my academic study of human beings tethered to the hard and beautiful reality of lived relationships. While we were expecting our second child, Jonathan, we moved to Atlanta, where I began doctoral work in the marvelously open, stimulating, and collegial environment of Emory University's Graduate Division of Religion. From the outset

I was given the freedom to frame my work there in terms of the model of sacrificial love and listening that was emerging as the guiding motivation for my studies. One of the many professors who participated in my first-semester seminar on method and theory asked the class to read Robert Wuthnow's analysis of how survey participants retold Jesus' parable of the Good Samaritan, and as I pondered that story anew, I realized that it addressed many of the moral and intellectual challenges that beset my project of knowing and loving Muslims. In an attempt to bring my religious motivations into conversation with the class, I decided to write my term paper as a commentary on Luke 10:25-37. The gist of that essay—remembered now through the lens of much subsequent reflection—was roughly as follows.

In answer to his own question about how to inherit eternal life, the legal scholar to whom Jesus addresses the parable begins by citing the command to "love the Lord your God with all your heart and with all your soul and with all your strength and with all your mind." What better introduction to a young scholar's effort to integrate his intellectual pursuits into a whole and undivided life of devotion to God? This command compels me to ask what it might mean to study Islam as an act of love for God. It does not even begin to answer that question, however. All it tells me is that the ultimate purpose of my scholarship cannot be merely to satisfy some human curiosity or desire or even need, nor can its method or its success be judged simply by how well it fulfills such humanistic ends.

The law's second demand is to "love your neighbor as yourself." How can scholarship fulfill that mandate? For the natural sciences, this imperative appears to demand a concern for human welfare. It does not require Christians to focus exclusively on applied sciences with evident social benefits, but it does seem to call for scholarship that engages other human beings in selfless ways—that supports, encourages, challenges, and serves other scientists or even the broader public, rather than just gratifying the scholar's personal curiosity or ambition. The increasingly interdependent and collaborative nature of scientific research appears in this respect a salutary development that Christians can support, and in which they should set the standard for selflessness. For the social sciences, this command raises forcefully the question of whether it is morally justifiable to regard the people one studies as objects of knowledge, upon whom one looks down from the vantage point of disciplinary expertise, rather than as interlocutors and knowers on a level with oneself. For the humanities, this command suggests a re-centering from the traditional humanistic project of forming and expanding the Self and its own culture, to what we might call the inter-humanistic goal of understanding and serving the Other.

Those of us who inhabit the Western humanistic tradition, and those of us who constitute the Church, have often fallen into the trap of loving our non-Western or non-Christian neighbors not exactly "as ourselves," but "as potentially like ourselves"—as potential converts to Christianity, or as still imperfect mirrors of Western culture, rather than as selves worth knowing and loving for their own sake. For my study of Islam, the command to love my neighbor as myself means that my scholarship must model and promote interpersonal relationships in which the Other is loved for who she is, without regard for whether she fits my hopes or serves my agenda. That requires a relentless and sacrificial pursuit of understanding, so that the person I love is really the Other and not a projection of myself. At the same time it requires integrity on my part, so that it is really my own self, and not some watered down accommodation of myself to the Other, who knows, engages, and loves the Other. Therefore, I will not judge my scholarship on Islam to be successful because it leads to better predictions of human behavior, more universal generalizations about human nature, or more nuanced classifications of human thought. I will judge it to be successful if and only if, in retrospect, it proves to have embodied and enabled human relationships characterized by love, integrity, and an ongoing process of coming to understand the Other. Only if my scholarship fulfills God's command to love my neighbor as myself can it fulfill the command to love God with my whole heart, soul, strength, and mind.

One drawback of directing my scholarship toward the cultivation of interpersonal relationships is that this may cause me to overlook the way religion operates at the level of groups and institutions. In the essay I wrote for my first-year methods seminar, I acknowledged this pitfall, but went on to argue that interpersonal relationships are an adequate guiding metaphor for scholarship because the moral demands imposed upon us by social structures are reducible, in principle, to the ethics of interpersonal relations. Though I harbored some doubts about this claim, I chose to orient my scholarship around what seemed to me the most fundamental moral demand of all, the duty to love my individual neighbor. Rather than just staking out this position as a personal faith-based assumption, however, I was able to point out that this focus on interpersonal relationships was also very much in sympathy with some of the secular theorists we had read for the seminar. The ritual theorist Catherine Bell, for example, questioned the longstanding tendency in religious studies to analyze power at the level of structures and institutions, because she felt this obscured or denied the moral agency of individuals. I was not as concerned as she to empower individuals, but my goal of understanding them gave me a similar motivation to attend to the particular ways in which individuals interpret, resist, suffer, negotiate, and recreate the power relations in which they find themselves. My attempt to ground my methodology in a Gospel parable did not cut me off from my secular colleagues; it allowed me to participate with them, from a distinctively Christian perspective, in a shared project and concern.

Jesus' interlocutor finds himself somewhat embarrassed by the high bar he has just set for inheriting eternal life, so he proceeds to inquire just how close to himself a person must be to constitute his neighbor. In its original context in Leviticus 19:18, the command to "love your neighbor as yourself" appears to have in view fellow Israelites, but Jesus' parable shows that the questioner's neighbor is not those in closest proximity to him—the priest and the Levite—but rather the victim, who represents powerlessness and need, and also the Samaritan, who represents social and religious distance. The neighbors whom this parable calls me to love and understand are not those most like myself, but Others, including most especially the outsider, the needy, and the vulnerable. As pointed out repeatedly in the methods seminar, however, the history of Western understanding of Others—especially Others whom we regard as in need of our help—is fraught with moral ambivalence. More often than not, Westerners and Christians have invented inferior Others as mirror images of themselves, to use in their own reflections on their own identities. Others are especially easy to objectify and use in this way, for merely to call someone an Other is to choose to regard him in light of the distance that separates us, while choosing to overlook the commonalities that make us moral and intellectual peers. Among the readings for our seminar was an essay in which the feminist anthropologist Lila Abu-Lughod attacked the dichotomy between Self and Other, and the use of Others in constructing the Self, as irretrievably implicated in Western colonialism and racism. My commentary on Luke's parable acknowledged the risk of self-serving objectification, but argued that identifying and constructing Muslims as religious Others does not inevitably reduce them to objects of our own mental manipulations. On the contrary, by calling for relationship as the primary response to Otherness, I was putting myself in substantial sympathy with Abu-Lughod's insistence that "we are always part of what we study and we always stand in definite relations to it."[1] The command to love Others "as yourself" provides just the kind of moral challenge that a critical scholar like Abu-Lughod might be able to appreciate: the challenge to love Others as ourselves without assimilating them to ourselves—to know them as independent agents on a level with ourselves and in relation to ourselves, without denying the Otherness that makes us enigmas to one another.

The command to love those different from myself raised for me once again the question of whether it is actually possible to understand someone else's religious experience. Must Others always remain to some degree an enigma to me? One of our seminar readings was a prepublication draft of Paul

---

1   Lila Abu-Lughod, "Can There Be a Feminist Ethnography?" *Women and Performance* 5 (1990): 27.

Griffiths' *Religious Reading,* in which he argued that since being religious involves giving an account that seems both comprehensive and unsurpassable, it is impossible for me to experience what it is like to belong to a different religion without first abandoning my own. If this is so—and I am not inclined to dispute it—then how can I hope to ever understand a religious Other as she understands herself? I cannot. At this point, however, defining the ultimate goal of religious studies as the cultivation of a certain kind of interpersonal relationship turns out to be most salutary. For a relationship to be characterized by love, integrity, and an ongoing process of coming to understand, it need not ever achieve full phenomenological understanding of the Other's experience. If the goal of scholarship is just loving human interaction, then scholars have no need to pursue anything more than the kind of knowledge that is necessary for and derived from ordinary human interaction. In a healthy friendship, for example, we do not expect to reach a state of perfected understanding; rather, we expect an ongoing dialectic in which each party forms an understanding of the other sufficient to permit productive interaction, and then repeatedly revises that understanding in response to misunderstandings and breakdowns in the relationship. That our understanding of other human beings always remains tentative and flawed is only a failure if the goal of religious studies is some kind of objective description, classification, explanation, or prediction of religious phenomena; if the goal is ethical human relationships, then understanding need never be final or complete. Indeed, healthy relationships require that understanding remain always subject to revision. My doubts about the impossibility of fully knowing another human being were not overcome by Jesus' parable, but they were put in perspective: since the goal of scholarship is not knowledge itself, but love, the only kind of knowledge I seek is that which enables love.

The alternative to loving my neighbor is to refuse the imperative of relationship by "passing by on the other side" of the road, as the priest and the Levite did. This has been a temptation for the Western Church, which has often retreated from the challenge of relationship with Muslims into the comfort of imagining Islam as a legalistic or violent antithesis to Christianity. Refusing relationship is also a temptation for scholars of religion who have been trained to look down on the objects of their study from a higher plane of objective or critical distance, rather than engaging them as peers from whom they might actually learn something. Many of us were taught that critical study means adopting a hermeneutic of suspicion: never accepting at face value what religious people tell us about themselves, but always seeking to debunk their myths, explain away their experiences, or unmask the oppression they have clothed with piety. Now, I do not deny that suspicion is sometimes warranted even in a loving relationship. A friend who believes all the self-serving tales we spin about ourselves, and never challenges our motives or our self-understanding, is a poor friend indeed. But scholarly critique, like the incisive questioning of a trusted friend, is not a project one may engage in for one's own gratification, for the satisfaction of unmasking another's sin. Criticism cannot be an end in itself. If it constitutes just one moment in an ongoing dialectic, in which the Other is allowed to object and to question my critical analysis, then it may be an act of love even if it meets with resistance and anger. But if it unilaterally cuts off the very relationship it is intended to serve, dismissing the Other's response as irrelevant to the scholar's project, then it is incompatible with God's command to love my neighbor as myself. If my recent book on the history of Islamic hermeneutical theories leads to an impasse in my attempt to converse with certain Muslim intellectuals, because it suggests that their preferred hermeneutic was invented to let them interpret the Qur'an any way they like, it may still prove in retrospect to have been an important step in a longer-term relationship—but only if my next book takes Muslim responses into account, and reframes my critical probing in such a way that my interlocutors are able to respond.

Rather than passing by on the other side, the Good Samaritan chooses to bind himself to the needy Other in a relationship that is compassionate, costly, and open-ended, bandaging his wounds and pledging his own purse to cover the cost of his continued care. His example demands of me a life-long, open-ended, and selfless commitment to cultivating relationships with my Muslim neighbors through scholarship. It also directs me down specific methodological paths. In my essay, the Good Samaritan's example led me to affirm several of the developments in the humanities that my professors had affirmed during the methods seminar. First, it led me to assert that historical, textual, and functional analysis of religion should always remain subservient to a semiotic or hermeneutical project like the anthropology of Clifford Geertz, which was oriented toward understanding symbol systems for the ultimate purpose of being able to converse with the people who inhabit them. Second, it led me to affirm an emerging trend in religious studies away from the old focus on the central elements of religious traditions, and toward the boundaries and interactions between them. I have pursued this emphasis in my research on the interpretation of Scriptures across religious lines, especially Muslim studies of the Bible. The Good Samaritan's model of relationship also sealed my commitment to the new trend in religious studies toward making public the values that guide one's scholarship. If a healthy human relationship is a two-way street, then relating to the people I study means disclosing myself just as much as it means getting to know them.

In concluding his parable, Jesus inverts the question of who is my neighbor. At first my neighbor seems to be the wounded Other who needs my help, but at the end of the parable my neighbor turns out to be the Good Samaritan himself—the Other who reaches out to help the man in need. This proved for me the most uncomfortable section of the parable. I was reaching out to my Muslim neighbors by devoting my career to them, but was I willing that they should reach out to me, help me, teach me, and contribute to God's work in my own life? If human relationships are necessarily reciprocal to some degree, could I expect the relationship between a Christian scholar and his Muslim subjects to remain strictly one–way? And what about my relationship to the secular academy and its discourses: was I here only to save them, or must I allow them to transform me? I had already begun to let that happen by allowing critical theory to shape my understanding of human depravity. About this time I read Miroslav Volf's Exclusion and Embrace, in which he argued that one's own identity must always remain open to being reshaped by interactions with Others. Would I allow the thought and voice of the Muslim Others I studied, and of the secular Others with whom I studied, to reshape not only my understanding of Muslims but also my understanding of myself and of my own scholarship? Would that make me less Christian, or more

Christ-like? I have gambled on the latter, following, I hope, the implications of Jesus' parable.

Surely I am not the only Christian to feel that letting my interactions with non-Christians redefine me threatens the sense of security and identity that my faith provides. That, however, is a discomfort I must be willing to accept. If loving my neighbor sacrificially enough to really engage her in conversation means loosening my grip on some cherished part of my own identity, so be it. The Kingdom of God does not depend on my sense of security in my own convictions; it is made visible as I love the one who opposes me, turn the other cheek even in debate, and learn poverty of spirit.

This does not mean that I must give up the content of my convictions. Attempting to understand and love Muslims has never led me to doubt or modify any particular article of Christian belief. On the contrary, the longer I study Muslim writings, the more I grieve at how far they are from the Gospel. I certainly see great logic, beauty, and dignity—as well as human sinfulness—in Islamic thought and life. In many ways Islam seems to me precisely the kind of religious system that I would have come up with myself, if I had been a virtuous and brilliant individual left to my own devices in the context of the late antique Near East. But it is a deeply human construct; it is, if anything, all too familiar. I have never felt it challenge my fallen human nature or my all-too-comfortable view of the world the way the Bible does day after day. Consequently, I have never felt any personal attraction to it.

On the other hand, if my identity as a Christian is constituted not only by the content of Christian belief, but also by how

I stand in relation to Others (as Miroslav Volf emphasizes), then I will repeatedly come to see the content of my faith in a new light, and relate to it in new ways, as I continue to interact with Muslims. One salient example of this in my own spiritual growth has been my study of Islamic hermeneutics. As I developed a critical eye for the kinds of self-serving interpretations of Scripture that some Islamic hermeneutical theories seemed designed to legitimate, I became more and more conscious of my own tendency toward self-gratification in my reading of the Bible, and of my own church's tendency to squeeze the Bible into a Reformed theological system. I do not despair of the Holy Spirit's ability to convict believers of such self-deception, nor have I given up Reformed theology as a powerful lens for understanding Scripture, but I do find myself chastened and humbled—still confident but less self-confident—in the convictions that I bring to my interactions with Muslims. One thing we always share with Others is our sinfulness, and if interacting with fallen Others makes us more conscious of our own fallenness, that makes us better Christians, not weaker ones.

Structuring my first seminar paper at Emory as an explicit exercise in obedience to Christ was something of a risk. Not that I feared exposing my faith; I feared I was being tacky and preachy about it. To my delight, however, the sociologist who read my paper loved it. He took it as a genuine engagement with the methodological issues raised in the methods seminar, and with the many faculty who had participated in the course—every one of whom figured somewhere in the paper. Apparently, I was speaking a language that was at once explicitly Christian and meaningful to my secular academic colleagues.

I later submitted that essay as a writing sample along with my application for a Harvey Fellowship, a graduate stipend offered by a Christian family foundation that aims to mark, equip and encourage graduate students at premier universities to actively integrate their faith and vocation as leaders in occupations where Christians are underrepresented. In my case, the Fellowship did just that. Even as I filled out the lengthy application, I solidified my commitment to pursuing my own vision and doing my own thing in the academy. I would continue to let my more secular colleagues shape and even direct my intellectual journey, but I knew where I was coming from, and I now had a pretty good idea of where I was going. There would be no turning back.

3. Listening to Muslims

Articulating moral and methodological principles at an abstract level is one thing. Figuring out what they might entail for the daily work of scholarship took me a little longer. It began in that same first-year seminar at Emory, when a Hebrew Bible student inadvertently set my research agenda by asking me one day "How do Muslims study the Bible?" All I knew to answer was that they usually don't, because they regard it as an unreliable record of what the prophets Moses, David, and Jesus actually taught. I realized at once, however, that this could not be the whole story. Surely many Muslims throughout history had found all kinds of things to say about the Bible, and if I was studying Islam for the purpose of enhancing my ability to converse with Muslims, what better way than to study Muslim perspectives on my own Scripture?

I began to dig, and discovered some forgotten century–old scholarship on Islamic versions of "the Psalms of David." It took another decade, however, before I finally published an analysis of that tradition of rewritten Psalms manuscripts, because in the meantime my advisor redirected me. He suggested that before I try to understand Muslim interpretations of the Bible, I ought perhaps to get a handle on how Muslims interpret the Qur'an. My dissertation, accordingly, was on early Islamic hermeneutical theories.

Studying Western and Islamic hermeneutical theories comparatively raised again quite forcefully the problem of how human beings understand each other. For one thing, I could not find any classical Islamic discourse that addressed the questions of modern Western hermeneutics in any depth. As I sat through lecture after lecture on the interpretation of imperative verbs or plural nouns, during a semester studying traditional legal theory in Morocco, I began to despair of finding anything but the most simplistic grammatical analysis of language and meaning. My frustration mounted. Why should it take an hour and a half to explain that "horses" refers to an entire class of beings, whereas "a horse" refers to just one individual from that class? If I was to avoid joining a long tradition of condescending Western scholarship on the simple-mindedness of Islamic religious thought, I had assume that it was I, not my teacher, who was missing something.

I was; but to find out what I was missing, I had to deconstruct my conception of hermeneutics. On the surface, Muslim legal theorists and modern Western theorists of language and interpretation appeared to be talking about entirely different things, and it took several years of picking sentence by sentence through arcane arguments before I was able to express Western questions about language and meaning in classical Islamic terms, and vice versa. Gradually I became convinced that Muslim interpreters of the Qur'an and Western philosophers were both up against the same vexing problem that I had encountered earlier in my study of critical theory: humans are astonishingly adept at interpreting texts, data, and people to suit their own agendas, and hermeneutical theories tend to mask or legitimate such self-serving forms of understanding.

This was not just an observation about how Muslims interpret scripture; it also called into question my own attempts to understand Muslims. Was I just forcing Islamic legal theorists to answer my modern Western hermeneutical questions, manipulating them into the conversation partners that my scholarly and moral objectives required? How could I be sure that I was really understanding them, and getting to know them rather than just myself? I found a way out of this skepticism thanks to Ludwig Wittgenstein and the cross of Christ. I encountered Wittgenstein's later writings in my college philosophy classes, and then again at Emory through the formative experience of reading Anthony Thiselton's New Horizons in Hermeneutics. Wittgenstein convinced me that if we are able to know when human communication is succeeding, and when we are understanding one another, this is not because of any stable or universal linguistic structures, but only because verbal communication takes place within the larger context of lived interaction. We know when language is being used and understood correctly because we live and interact with others in ways that are not merely verbal but also practical and concrete, and we have common expectations and make shared judgments about when this interaction is successful and when it fails. Buying a house, for instance, is a highly symbolic affair that hinges on signed pieces of paper covered with words and numbers. The reason we all agree that this symbolic interaction has succeeded is that when I move into my new house, the previous residents, who the day before would have fought me tooth and nail to keep me out, put up no resistance to my invading their home. Those signed pieces of paper—or, more precisely, the rule–governed rituals of signing them—have dramatic practical effects because they are part of a very practical and concrete game that we all agree to play. The practical success of lived human interaction is what gives cash value to the paper money of language, and reassures us that communication is actually taking place.

Given my commitment to human relationships, I appreciated Wittgenstein's appeal to the lived interaction within which verbal communication takes place. Understanding does not happen simply at the level of ideas conveyed by words; it is a product of interactions that are physical as well as verbal, and if physical interaction succeeds in generating concrete physical or economic goods, then surely verbal communication is succeeding by at least one very important measure. Nevertheless, I had been learning to be skeptical of practical success. Both critical theory and Reformed theology reminded me that I always measure success in relation to my own needs and aims. I do not want to judge how well I understand people by how successfully I am able to manipulate them into serving my own ends! Jesus' Sermon on the Mount, and its perfect expression in Jesus' glorification on the cross, suggested a different criterion: perhaps I know that I am really coming to understand another person in the way love

assumptions and values of their Muslim authors. Studying the texts in preparation for each class was like getting to know a perplexing but fascinating new friend. When I arrived in class, however, and tried to share that sense of discovery with my students, I felt that it had become as dry as dust, and my students often agreed. Eventually I discovered why: it was not the conclusions of my study that really captivated me, but the process of interpretation itself.

This discovery led me to try something that seemed to me quite radical: instead of writing out in advance the insights I wanted to convey to students, I wrote out the questions I would ask them about the readings, and left the conclusions in their hands. I tried to limit my role to asking questions, structuring discussion around their observations and interpretations, and taking notes so that I could write up our conclusions and post them online after class. I had never seen anyone attempt such a reversal—writing the lecture, in effect, after the class. But my philosophy of religious studies seemed to require it. If the purpose of religious studies was to learn to listen to Muslims, and ultimately to come to know and love them, then I needed to let my students do that for themselves. Furthermore, if teaching, like scholarship, is first and foremost a form of human relationship, then it too needs to be characterized by sacrificial listening. My own theory demanded that I listen to my students, discern their categories and questions, and make their concerns my own, just as I had learned to care about the theological struggles of Muslim intellectuals.

Putting this pedagogy into practice was nerve–wracking. I lost much of my control, not only over the conclusions we reached, but also over the success of the class. If students were not well prepared, or did not have the tenacity to bear with a tedious theological treatise, the class was a miserable failure, and there was precious little I could do about it. The sense of competence that had sustained me perhaps too much during graduate school was gone. Student evaluations fluctuated from euphoric to dismal from one semester to the next. But I was finally doing something that made sense to me. I was helping students to construct their own understandings of Muslims, through their own careful listening to Muslim voices. I might often fail. Indeed, I found that I had to give up the desire for success as a teacher, and be willing to risk failure, so that my students could succeed as students. Most universities and teaching consultants stress the quality of teaching, but I suspect that this language sends us down the wrong path. It now seems to me necessary, though exceedingly difficult, to pry my mind away from trying to be a good teacher and focus on helping my students to be good students. Teaching is not about me. In fact, it is not really about my students either. According to my theory of religious studies, the whole point of teaching is to take the focus off both teacher and student, and listen, as attentively and sacrificially as we can, to the Muslim authors we are reading.

I now refer to this teaching method as "a pedagogy of sacrificial listening." As I tell students at the beginning of each term, I don't want them to come away with "talking knowledge"—the ability to say intelligent things about Islam. I want them to gain "listening knowledge"—the ability to hear what Muslims are saying, interpret it in terms of their own mental, moral, and religious categories, and then listen again until their interpretations start to break down and they are forced to modify their categories and try again. This is, by its nature, a frustrating process. We love clarity, so we are quick to pigeon-hole people based on our first impressions. We are happiest if we can keep people in the boxes we construct for them, interpreting everything they do and say to fit our prior impressions of them, whether those be positive or negative. Sacrificial listening means committing to get to know people for who they are, not who we want them to be, and that means constantly questioning our interpretations, so that we spend most of the semester in unsettled confusion. As I tell every class on day one, this kind of study requires moral commitment, because it will not always be fun or even interesting. Nor would I want it to be, even if I had the rhetorical skills to make it entertaining. If the Gospel is true, then teaching and learning, like scholarship, art, and perhaps even business, are fundamentally about redemptive suffering.

5. Conclusion

As I reflect today on the present state of my pedagogy and research, I see above all the need to let them be shaped by the agendas of three groups of Others. One group of Others whom I face every day are my students, and I am slowly learning to let their questions and interests shape the questions I ask in class. I now begin each semester spending at least two class sessions trying to discern and articulate what concerns and presuppositions the students are bringing with them. They are often not at all the concerns that most engage my mind, and sometimes I wonder how we can possibly use a semester of reading Islamic theological texts to address their presentist concerns about media stereotypes or "the Islamic threat." But if scholarship is a relationship that requires sacrificing my own agendas so that I can discern those of the people I study and thus enter into a genuine conversation with them, then teaching is also a relationship, and it will require sacrificing my own intellectual proclivities so that the conversation in the classroom can genuinely include not just me and the Muslim authors, but the students as well. That is what the cross of Christ means for me today in my teaching.

A second group of Others is the secular academy, of which I am a full member, but within which I have marked out a decidedly Christian space. I do not believe that my Christian presuppositions and concerns make my work irrelevant to non-Christian scholars. My moral concerns about the possibility of human communication and the ethics of human relationship are shared by numerous scholars in many disciplines, from critical theorists to the many old-fashioned liberal Protestants and humanists who still constitute a majority in the field of religious studies. What distinguishes me from most of them is that I seek the answer to these dilemmas not in an academic elite's ability to prescribe and manage the relationships between religious people so that no one's rights are violated, but precisely in giving up our rights and interests, and in letting our relationship with the Other be shaped by the interests and objectives of that Other. Everyone but the starkest skeptic or the most unabashed egoist aspires to understanding, but I believe it can only be found through a self-sacrificial model of scholarship as listening. The language of sacrifice is rooted in my Christian faith—in the Parable of the Good Samaritan, the Sermon on the Mount, and the Cross of Christ—and though that language may be unique in some ways, it resonates with many of the concerns and hopes of non-Christians as well. My challenge now is to take that language of sacrificial listening and translate it into terms that will make sense to others in my field and perhaps beyond it. That will require years of new study, reading non-Christian thinkers like Emmanuel Levinas who have wrestled with similar issues, and allowing those thinkers to reshape the way I express and even the way I conceptualize what the Gospel has to offer by way of hope and methodology for the secular academy.

My third group of Others are today's Muslim intellectuals. A defining moment in my relationship with this far-flung and diverse community was a comment I received on a graduate seminar paper on Ibn Taymiyya's theory of Islamic politics. My professor, a prominent Muslim scholar of constitutional law deeply concerned with human rights and the reformation of Islamic law, asked how my purely historical study could help him in his efforts to change Islamic law today. I had not set out to help Muslim intellectuals in their endeavors; indeed that would have been viewed by many of my teachers as a betrayal of scholarly objectivity. But my professor's comment confronted me with the fact that Muslims are not just the thinkers I study, they are my academic colleagues. My scholarship should and does contribute to their thinking as much as it does to my more secular colleagues; indeed I have an even greater responsibility to them, if I want my scholarship to be a form of relationship rather than an attempt at objective analysis engaged in from some supposedly higher plane of academic discourse. Learning to listen to my Muslim neighbors is all very noble, but listening by itself does not constitute a relationship; that requires a conversation, to which I must be willing to contribute my own insights with integrity and transparency.

My professor's question prompted me to see even my most nitty-gritty historical scholarship in a new light: it is not the end result of my attempt to understand, but just one moment in an ongoing conversation, not only with other historians of Islamic thought, but also with living Muslims. What their response will be to my most recent book I hardly dare to think. It is historical, but it is not without provocative language and implications that challenge traditional ways of imagining Islamic law. I would not have made its critical implications so explicit in the conclusion if engaging contemporary Muslim intellectuals were not one of my main goals. Such a thoughtful challenge can be a perfectly legitimate part of a healthy human relationship; it may even be a sign of just how carefully I have listened to Muslim scholars. But if it leads only to alienation, it will have failed. I cannot force my Muslim interlocutors into a relationship; but if relationship is my goal, then I must be willing to leave a closed door behind and knock at another one. If my scholarship is to be an exercise in sacrificial listening for the sake of human relationships characterized by integrity and an ongoing process of coming to understand Others, then I must be willing to refine, revise, or even give up some of the conclusions that I reached with such conviction in my book on the formation of Islamic hermeneutics. I must remember that the purpose of that book is just to enable one further step in a life-long conversation. If continuing that conversation requires changing the nature of the questions I ask, renegotiating the conceptual vocabulary with which I answer them, or even discovering that I was just plain wrong, then holding onto the conclusions I labored so hard to produce would be the kind of scholarship that only serves to protect the scholar's own sense of identity and self-righteousness. If my identity and righteousness are found in Christ, and in his self-sacrificial act of taking on a particular human identity and then giving up that life to the violence of those he came to serve, then my own intellect will have to be reshaped and renegotiated through my interactions with Muslims. That, rather than any fixed and preformulated way of thinking about Islam or hermeneutics, is what will make my knowledge of Muslims truly Christian. Indeed, a willingness to sacrifice our own most precious conclusions may be a necessary trait of all truly Christian scholarship.

Such scholarship cannot but be a painful process. Scholarship that is characterized by genuine listening, and by a process of coming to understand other human beings, may be momentarily exhilarating and satisfying, but it must be enduringly difficult. How could one pursue such a path without the hope of the Gospel, which turns suffering itself into abiding joy? It is not in our nature. I do not see how my secular colleagues could do it. Indeed I do not see how I can do it. But God transforms and empowers us in mysterious ways—not least of which is the communion of other redeemed sinners like those represented in this book, who are striving to glimpse God's glory in the various vocational struggles to which they are called.

Art Identity: Christian. Artist. Stranger.

Sarah Awad
Los Angeles, CA
USA

1. Introduction

The art world has long been a part of culture devoid of an active and influential Christian presence. Compound this lack with the uncomfortable place the art world holds in modern Christendom and the result is a territory rife with challenges for the practicing Christian–professional artist. Among these challenges, we face the trial of loneliness, a common experience for all Christians of simply being an alien in the world in which we exist but to which we do not belong.

More specific challenges that come with functioning as a Christian in the arts include the challenge of living a divided life, dealing with ambition, combating bitterness, and working through self-doubt. Through each one of these challenges, we find an opportunity to know ourselves better and to know

God better. In having to reconcile a divided life, we can realize the fullness of our identity as artists through Christ. In having to face our ambition, we can discover the importance of a successful private life. In having to deal with our bitterness, we can gain an awareness of how to understand ourselves rightly. And in having to contend with self-doubt, we can learn the necessity of maintaining mission.

2. Identity: Christian. Artist. Stranger.

As a Christian artist, I often feel torn between the two aspects of my identity. Being a Christian and being an artist requires active participation in very discrete communities (professional and personal), thus keeping my two selves moderately segregated. Simply put, the challenge for a Christian artist is how to live as an integrated person – a person of faith who is intellectually curious, politically critical, and creatively motivated.

Tensions arise when I try to behave as 'the artist' in the Christian community or 'the Christian' in the artist community. The Christian community expects that most art will be subversive, morally degrading, and divergent from revelations of truth or beauty. The art community expects that Christians will be conservative, judgmental, and here's the real kicker, that art made by Christians will be trite, cliché, and heavy handedly evangelistic. These may sound like offensive over-generalizations, but speak to anyone in the Christian circles about their personal experiences of contemporary art and you will inevitably hear language such as "dark," "demonic," and "perverse" used to describe what they have seen. (I believe this arises as much from a general lack of understanding of how to look at contemporary art that pervades the American public, as from misconceptions within the church.) Speak to educators in the art community and you will inevitably hear stories of frustration with students who see their faith-based art as a tool for classroom evangelism. The divergent world-views and misunderstandings between the two communities make it difficult to function as the same person in both sets of circumstances.

Of all the misconceptions that Christians hold about con-temporary art perhaps the most disconcerting is the need to evaluate its goodness and/or validity based on its relevance to the kingdom of God. I am not sure where this notion comes from. We certainly do not judge everything by this standard. For example, it would be absurd if we evaluated sporting events based on their service to the kingdom of God. And yet, this prejudice is placed on art, perhaps because we consider creativity to be a spiritual act, likening it to the acts of God our creator. While the creative act certainly has a spiritual component, attempting to understand every artwork based on this rubric poses certain problems.

First off, the concern of whether or not an artwork is "good" is not really a pertinent conversation in the contemporary art world. Most artists recognize that taste drives the reception of art. Because of its subjective nature, taste is a poor tool with which to evaluate art. The meaning of art is constructed, translated through experience, and subjective, based on the context in which it is received.

Saying that taste is relative does not eliminate the need for criticality. Rather it should shape the way we look at art. By participating in the contemporary art world, artists invite the public to critically engage with their work. As viewers, we should ask ourselves what a particular artwork is doing and how/why it is doing it. But the underlying and unstated question that many people bring to an artwork is not "what is it doing?" but "is it doing what I think it should be doing?", thus bringing the strong bias of the viewer to the work. I am not suggesting that we assume ourselves to be neutral beings, but that we take into account our biases as we critically engage with the work.

When I teach students to look at art, the first question I ask them is "what is it?" By this, I do not mean 'what do you think you see?' but 'what do you actually see?'. This question often refers to the material nature of the object, its formal aspects, asking the students to examine the historical, sociological, psychological meaning behind every decision the artist has made. From this we can construct our understanding of the meaning of the work, what it is actually doing. But too often, as uneducated or lazy viewers, when we ask "what is it?" we are asking the easier and more representational version of that question; by asking, "what is it? what do I see?" we are asking "what does it look like?". A clear example of this comes with the territory of contemporary painting. A viewer's initial response of "what is it?" does not mean "what kind of painting is it?" (referring to all the historical, cultural, and psychological meaning behind the marks or decisions of the artist, from the actual formal application of paint to the support on which it is made – i.e. large wooden panel vs. cut up found objects, etc.) Rather, the question means, "Is that a painting of …?" (referring to what it represents – i.e. is that a painting of a chicken?) Representational imagery often does constitute a large part of the work, but when we as viewers immediately give preference to those concerns over others, we lose a lot of the potential meaning of the work.

The tragedy of the public's experience with contemporary art is that many find it difficult to understand. But just because something is obscure or mysterious or difficult to relate to does not necessarily translate it as being bad or not worth looking at. In fact, while many viewers desire clarity, wishing to be told directly what the artist is thinking about, most artists value complicated, nuanced and often obscure readings of their work, knowing that it is often through an indirect path or journey that truth can be understood.

This way of looking at art can change the way we evaluate whether or not it is good. It is no longer a question of whether or not the art does what we think it should do. We can be critical of art based on an entirely new set of compelling rules/ philosophies, which are shaped by our own point of view (which can include but is not limited to our spiritual perspective) and influenced by other writers, artists, thinkers, etc.

This idea that art should be judged based on its spiritual relevance or adherence to Christian virtues places Christian artists in an awkward position. For one, it alienates Christian artists from the rest of the art world. More importantly, it asks Christians to rationalize their artistic ambition by claiming evangelism as a creative motivation. We ask Christian artists to justify their desire for public recognition of their work by prioritizing its ability to bring more people into the kingdom of God. In *Art Needs No Justification*, H.R. Rookmaaker describes art that is used as an evangelistic tool as often being debased to propaganda. A more subtle justification that we ask Christian artists to make is that as long as the work was made in order to glorify God, then the artist's feelings about personal achievement are beyond reproach. First, can we not say if we are living by faith in alignment with God, then all that we do is for the glory of God – whether singing a song in church, making a work of art, or drinking orange juice? For a Christian, the sacred cannot be separated from the secular. So the question of whether or not a work of art made by a Christian glorifies God should not really be an issue. So much of the Christian life is not really about what we choose to do, but the person we choose to be while we do it. Therefore, if I choose be a person who seeks and obeys God, then I don't need evangelism to justify my art.

In today's church, art is primarily seen as an evangelistic tool or a method for worship. Many churches have begun to en-courage all members to access their creative nature in order to better seek or relate to God. However, this ignores the pos-sibility of art as a profession. In fact, as a professional artist it is neither my desire to engage with the art world through evangelism nor to make artwork that is limited to conversa-tions within the Christian community. My primary interests lie in contributing to and participating in the dialogue gener-ated from an international community of artists making and exhibiting work. I believe this artistic motivation completely coincides with my understanding of my purpose from my creator.

Isaiah 43:10-13 states " 'You are my witnesses, ' declares the Lord, 'and my servant whom I have chosen, so that you may know and believe me and understand that I am he. Before me no god was formed, nor will there be one after me. I, even

I, am the Lord, and apart from me there is no savior. I have revealed and saved and proclaimed – I, and not some foreign god among you. You are my witnesses,' declares the Lord, 'that I am God." I was made to know God, through revelation and salvation. I am a living witness to who God is by virtue of being in a relationship with Him. Knowing God imbues everything else that I do with purpose. In particular, I see the creative process of thinking and making as one of many ways that I seek truth through critical engagement with the world.

It is rare to meet other active Christians (by that I refer to men and women who are actively engaged in life with God through faith) who are also actively involved in the arts, particularly at high levels. Unfortunately, our current social climate breeds an inversely proportional relationship: the longer you are involved with the arts, and the higher you rise in its hierarchies, the less likely you are to continue to engage your faith at the same level. Success in the art world often, but not always, involves moral compromise. More importantly, practicing art requires constant engagement with the ruling relativistic philosophies, which scorn Judeo-Christian teachings. Thus, Christian artists feel very acutely the strangeness of being a stranger in both worlds.

For a long time I have viewed the two distinct parts of my identity, Christian and artist, as being separate and equal. Like a wrestling match between similarly ranked opponents, I am never sure which one will gain the upper hand. But recently, I have come into a new ontological understanding – that God first and foremost forms my identity. The only way I can truly know who I am is through knowing God. Ontologically, we are not fixed beings. As we grow and change, we are constantly searching for a deep understanding of self, or trying to connect with our true selves. If I believe that God created me and knows me perfectly, then it is only through relationship with God, that I can come to understand the "self" He saw when He made me. In this way, through the working out of faith (Phil 2:12), we become who we were made to be. Therefore, the two competing parts of my life aren't necessarily in competition at all, but rather both fall under submission to the larger understanding of my personhood as determined by God. What I mean is this: It is through faith in God that I come to know how to live the life of a Christian and it is also through faith in God that I come to know how to live the life of an artist.

3. Integrity: Public Life with an Inward Gaze

Pursuit of a profession in the arts brings up certain conflicts with the model of faith presented in Scripture. Although I address this as one in the visual arts, these conflicts are no different from any other performance driven field. Perhaps the most obvious struggle is ambition or the desire for fame. Ambition essentially refers to a commitment to one's desires for personal achievement. Often this involves the public realm – a desire for affirmation or approval from one's peers and achieving recognition for one's work. So much of an artist's career involves the shaping of his/her reputation (through where the work gets shown, who sees it, who writes about it, who buys it, thereby establishing its market value, etc). Being an artist requires a certain amount of ambition or ego, otherwise one would never undertake the risk that is required to live the lifestyle. Artists must have enough confidence in their artistic vision to believe that it is worth the effort of making and presenting it to the public.

For a Christian artist, this ambition for public recognition appears directly opposed to the idea of humbling oneself before God. Through Scripture, we understand that we should desire to live a life of humility following the example of Jesus, who "being in very nature God did not consider equality with God something to be grasped" (Phil 2). We might take this to mean that to be a Christian we must not care how other people perceive us. We must not shape our reputation or seek professional visibility. Yet, there is scriptural evidence to support the opposite. Jesus himself gave us a model for being aware of one's public reputation and actively shaping it. As Jesus' public ministry increased, he became protective of how word of his miracles spread. Jesus kept his missional goals a priority and the outward manifestations of his ministry secondary (Mark 1:32-39). In the same way, an understanding of our professional goals (personal, communal, pedagogical) will help us determine where and how our work needs to be presented. Moreover, shaping a positive reputation for our personal character (through kindness, generosity, selflessness, graciousness, patience, confidence) is equally as important as gaining a positive perception of our work.

The reality of having to consider my public reputation was never more apparent in my life until this last year. While preparing a solo exhibition, a prime opportunity to craft a presentation of my work to the public, I experienced a painful rift in a friendship with an artist that resulted in my being accused of deceitfulness and greed. At the time, I set the broken relationship aside to literally focus on the work at hand: building a show that would reflect my artistic intentions, formulating an artist statement to accompany the paintings, and exercising other general forms of self-promotion. It took me months to realize that because of its spiritual implications, the way I handled that friendship would be infinitely more important for my future than a single solo show ever could be. It was probably the first time in my life I was placed in a situation where I felt I was so grievously wronged that I could not forgive. In fact, the point of frustration concerning this broken relationship was that some of my friend's accusations had become public and had the potential to influence my professional reputation. Only in the aftermath did I realize that instead of defending my public image, I needed to have a right heart. God challenged me with the radicalness of the Christian life, that we are defined by how we love our enemies. I believe that practicing forgiveness, a somewhat private matter of the heart, was just as valuable as all the work I put into creating a public exhibition.

As artists, it is right that we should care how we present ourselves professionally and there is wisdom in knowing how to navigate the public sphere. Again, Jesus sets a model for how to gain that wisdom. In the midst of his public ministry, Jesus took time out to meet with the Father. Early in the morning, he went to a solitary place to pray which gave him clarity of purpose so he could navigate the attention he was receiving (Mark 1:35-38). The challenges we face in the contemporary art world are numerous and complicated, from negotiating competing gallery interests to dealing with people using power and money to manipulate the market. How will we know how to behave and what decisions to make unless we are actively pursuing the Father's will through private prayer and listening?

As Christian artists, it is imperative that we find a balance between seeking professional visibility and laboring for greatness with God in private. The question we must always be willing to ask ourselves is what do we desire first, fame or God? And we must always be willing to give an honest answer. It is in the private places with God that we find the strength to live with integrity in public.

The only way to be successful publicly is to be successful privately. But we forget this. We focus on our public success because we think it is what matters the most and we think it is what we can control and ultimately what will make us happy. However, ambition for personal glory can never truly be satisfied. There is no substitute for a real intimate relationship with God. To desire God first means being able to pray: "Be Thou exalted over my reputation. Make me ambitious to please Thee even if as a result I must sink into obscurity and my name be forgotten as a dream. Rise, O Lord, into Thy proper place of honor, above my ambitions" (AW Tozer, Pursuit of God).

4. Humility: Knowing Oneself Rightly

Of all the challenges an artist faces, perhaps the most difficult is not growing bitter. If you are an artist long enough, you will inevitably experience the frustration of not achieving what you want and seeing your peers, both equal and lesser, promoted above you. The pain and resentment that comes from unmet expectations can cause bitterness to take deep root in our hearts. We can reject much of this bitterness by simply knowing who we are in Christ apart from comparing ourselves to other people. Galatians 6: 3-4 describes this type of humility: "If anyone thinks he is something when he is nothing, he deceives himself. Each one should test his own actions.

Then he can take pride in himself, without comparing himself to somebody else." If we judge our artistic achievements based on how we compare to those around us, we will never have a right view of ourselves. In fact, this kind of comparison can easily turn our genuine criticism of artistic endeavors into petty slander of our peers. Refraining from unnecessary gossip about other artists is easier when our hearts are free of bitterness and we are content with our own situation (which will inevitably be sometimes poor and sometimes plenty).

Inherent in making work for an audience is a willingness to subject it to public criticism. In these circumstances, it is difficult to separate rejection of one's work from rejection of one's self. If as an artist, your sole reason in submitting your work to the public is a desire for approval, you will cripple your potential for artistic growth.

When preparing my last exhibition, I was seized with a fear, not of how my work would be critically received, but simply of the judgment I anticipated from my peer group. A friend reminded me that in all actuality some of my friends would not like it and some of them would and that there would be the typical backbiting but also there would be back praising. This sage advice was to turn from what I could not control and instead, to focus my energy on making what I wanted to show and to be open to all kinds of conversations the work could generate. I have found that so much of exhibiting is about opening oneself up to the artistic dialogue. It is a chance to engage with my community. This means knowing what type of audience I want for my work and what I hope to gain from showing it. Hopefully, I can maintain the perspective that this gain goes beyond financial success or personal fame and instead involves contributing to a larger community.

It is common knowledge in the art world that rejection is not personal. In fact, rejection rarely even has anything to do the work of the artist. Many other factors contribute to rejection – you might not be making work that is sellable, fashionable, or of the particular taste of the person whose attention you seek. So much of the success of an artist's career is actually out of control of the hands of the artist. As a Christian, I have to trust that all the fortuitous circumstances and social relationships that appear as chance are really in the hands of God. Lay people always ask me if there are agents in the art world as there are in entertainment industry. That role doesn't really exist in any respected capacity, but I like to think of God as my personal agent. He can elevate me or advance my career as he sees fit. "For you died and your life is now hidden with Christ in God. When Christ, who is your life appears, then you also will appear with him in glory" (Col 3:3-4).

We cannot control the results of our labor but we can control the attitude by which we labor. Ecclesiastes 9: 10-11 says, "Whatever your hand finds to do, do it with all your might.... the race is not to the swift or the battle to the strong, nor does food come to the wise or wealth to the brilliant or favor to the learned; but time and chance happen to them all." Does the fact that our future is out of our control mean we should abandon our work? No. Instead, we are encouraged to pursue our labor with joy, to invest ourselves in the things we care about regardless of the results. According to Scripture, and despite what our parents have taught us, success or failure is not necessarily dependent on how strong or smart or educated we are. Rather our fate is in God's hands. Therefore, we should labor with a right attitude, without bitterness, resentment, or fear. As artists, we have the privilege of laboring for things of our choosing and we should make every effort to work with joy in the present and peace about the future.

5. Purpose: Maintaining Mission Rather Than Striving for Perfection

Even artists who care very little how the public receives their work still must grapple with artistic ambition. By this I refer to the impulse that drives the artist to make. In the artistic process there is always a point (often recurring) at which the question, "is this worth making?" arises. To proceed, the artist must overcome this self-doubt, sometimes by considering what is at stake – why make anything at all? Perhaps I have a desire for the work to have a powerful impact in my field, influencing generations of artists to come. Perhaps I desire the work to be serious, thoughtful, playful, communal, intellectually critical, or emotionally moving. Perhaps my motivation is a pursuit of pure aesthetic pleasure. Whatever the case, there is always a reason behind the making and if it isn't ambitious, then the result probably isn't worth looking at. The essence of being an artist involves discovering what compels me to think and to make. As a Christian, I must hold this creative motivation in proper relationship to my God-given purpose.

The common mythology surrounding artists is that the ego required is so great that there is no room for anything other than the artist himself. Making art requires focus, dedication and sometimes obsession. What is a necessary condition for the job can also be the most hazardous for our spiritual health. It becomes difficult to acknowledge God in his rightful place when we continue to serve art first on a daily basis. We deceive ourselves if we believe that our relationship to art will never become idolatrous. How often does our self-evaluation or emotional contentment depend on how well we performed an artistic task? When the creative process has that elusive quality of moving forward with purpose or accomplishment, we feel satisfied. However, when it feels slow, stilted, or stuck, we grow frustrated, as we believe this to be a reflection on our abilities as artists. At the end of the day, I can only leave my studio with a sense of well-being when I have made significant progress in my work. I am not saying that small studio successes are not necessary because, in fact, they are critical to a healthy studio practice. I am saying that we have to be careful about the source of our fulfillment. We enjoy our work because God has enabled us to do so. He is our source and He is the one we serve above all else. We must submit our pursuit of excellence in our craft and desire for artistic achievement under our desire for God.

Desiring God first is a crucial step to gaining artistic freedom. When we labor under the burden of achieving artistic greatness, fear of failure can prevent us from taking risks. However, we do not have to depend on our own judgment or the judgment of others to determine our sense of personal accomplishment. If God is the source of our approval then achieving greatness in our work need not define us. When we strive for greatness, we can do it out of a place of joy, satisfaction, and strength instead of neediness and vulnerability. When we are satisfied in God first, we can work with freedom from the weight of striving.

I do not think desiring God and being a working artist are at odds with one another. Because of the necessity of artistic ambition that drives the creative impulse, practicing faith and art together might look counter cultural, but the laying down of self in any area of life will always look counter cultural. It is in submitting our artistic ambition to our desire to know God that we discover how to truly be creatively ambitious and to work out our purpose as an artist.

Conclusion

Nathan Grills
University of Melbourne
Australia

David E. Lewis
Vanderbilt University
United States

S. Joshua Swamidass
Washington University, St. Louis
United States

Not to us, LORD, not to us
but to your name be the glory,
because of your love and faithfulness
Psalms 115:1 (NIV)

God wants all of our lives. This is the claim that began this
book. When God calls us to himself, he wants us to come to
him with everything that we are and aspire to be. This includes
our work. He wants control over our choice of profession, how
we do it, and how it fits in to the rest of our lives. Only He can

truly understand how our work fits into what He is doing in this world and through history. As John Stott has noted, "Every honorable work, whether manual or mental or both, whether waged or voluntary, however humble or menial, needs to be seen by Christians as some kind of cooperation with God, in which we share with him in the transformation of the world which he has made and committed to our care. This applies alike to industry and commerce, to public services and the professions, and to full-time home-making and motherhood" (Your Confirmation, 1991, 148).

How to be a professor, salesperson, or musician is part of the life of faith, not something off to the side. Additionally, how to be a Christian husband or wife, mother or father, or an active church member is equally important and is an area in which we should strive to achieve. Beyond our specific life of faith and work, God's redemptive work in humanity reaches to the professions in which many of us work. God wants to sanctify and renew our professions in the same way he wants to re-deem people and the other institutions that define human life. This edited collection was put together to help readers think about how different kinds of work fit into God's larger plan for his people. It is intended to help readers think about how to bring their work lives under God's direction and also how to sanctify the organizations, professions, and practices that define work.

So, what difference does it make that a person is a Christian in her profession? In our experience most Christians, if pressed, would suggest that being a Christian means that they try to love the people they encounter on the job and work with integrity. If Christian faith means anything in the workplace, it should definitely include these things. In our experience, however, there are plenty of kind, honest, and talented people in our professions that are not Christians. In fact, many of them are kinder, more honest, and more talented than we. Conversely, it is sometimes the unkind, discourteous and tricky that we later find out are 'Christians' when a non-Christian colleague remarks "…and do you know what? They call themselves a Christian!" To quote Mahatma Gandhi, when asked about Christianity spreading: "Oh, I don't reject Christ. I love Christ. It's just that so many of you Christians are so unlike Christ. If Christians would really live according to the teachings of Christ, as found in the Bible, all of India would be Christian today."

Where does this leave Christians? Is there anything distinctive about the presence of the Holy Spirit in our lives that marks us, that sanctifies our work? Certainly, the overwhelming love of Christ and its effects on us should be distinctive. In order for us to better understand what difference faith makes in our profession this book has collected the reflections of Christians working in diverse fields. The chapters are rich with insight derived from contemplation, and are grounded in experience, as authors discuss the integration of faith and work at a level deeper than many Christians have considered. The chapters speak to some common issues on this topic such as the mystery of calling, reconciling faith and ambition, and how God makes a difference in the substance and practice of specific professions. Collectively, the chapters provide examples of how faith and our work lives might be integrated beyond the common notions described above. More importantly, the chapters highlight just how easy it is to lose sight of what it means to be truly successful, successful in God's eyes. In this concluding chapter we revisit these themes, summarizing some key points and discussing the issues they raise.

1. Mystery of Calling

The chapters of this book focus on a deep and primary way that being a Christian can matter for work. The authors wrestle with the concept and practical implications of God's calling to enter a specific type of work or profession. The Scriptures make clear that God does call people to specific work. In 1 Corinthians 7 (NIV), Paul writes, "Only let each person lead the life that the Lord assigned to him, and to which God has called him." Paul uses the words 'assign' and 'call' in relation to work that most would normally refer to as secular. It is not only the missionary or church worker that is called by God to particular work. Rather, God calls people to work and professions in and out of the home and the church. The way that God cares for the world, for example, by providing it food, shelter, fellowship, and richness, is through the work of people who grow, transport, and sell food, build houses, form clubs, and make music and art and sport. This gives work inside and outside the church by believers and non-believers dignity and weight and importance. When people do this work, they participate with God in his continuing work of creation, care, and redemption.

Paul goes on to explain that all of the areas of our lives, including marital status, social position and work should be viewed from the perspective of how best to achieve God's glory. Our work, like other areas of our lives, should be understood in terms of how it can best glorify God (1 Cor 10:31; NIV). When Christians are confronted with commands like this one which suggest that God should have control over our choice of work and how it is to be done, they respond in different ways. Some Christians are unwilling to give God control over their work because their identity is so closely wrapped up in what they do. They have a hard time understanding how their lives could be valuable in some sort of meta sense apart from work in their professions. This is particularly true for Christians in prestigious professions. They have a hard time understanding how God could use them apart from what they do—design, medicine, or business. The risk is that they justify various sacrifices, some that even damage their relationship with Christ, in order to attain success in their work.

Ambition to succeed in their work or professions becomes the way some Christians attempt to serve God. The thinking behind this often looks something like this: "God has made me a public official/actor/academic and I am going to succeed in this business and this will bring glory to God. And, don't worry, I will be nice along the way and use my power and influence to help people." When professional success and spiritual success lie along the same path this may well bring God glory, but what about when the two diverge, as they likely will, does our faith still stand? Or are we tempted to help God out and compromise our families or cut corners to ensure our success and His glory? Some Christians are unable to entrust to God their professional trajectory, whether success or failure, and instead let their work career obsess them in the hope that the headlong pursuit of professional success and a robust life of faith are compatible. There is plenty in this book to suggest that a strongly held goal of professional success alongside a strongly held goal of following Christ is problematic. Too frequently it is unclear which goal is our real master and, as Jesus taught, we cannot serve two masters. When people hold tightly to their professional identity this is often a signal that work has supplanted God, the true master, and that a person looks to their profession to provide happiness, meaning and satisfaction, rather than to God himself.

Yet, this is only one side of the story. God does uniquely mark some persons for particular kinds of work and he desires that they do it excellently. In the same way that persons are called to full-time ministry, God has called others to specific professions that he will use for His purpose. An example of this concept can be found in the Old Testament where some were responsible for overseeing the work on the tabernacle and others leading the nation of Israel (Ex 35; NIV; 1 Sam 16; NIV). Both were ultimately for God's glory. For some, the calling is clear and easy to discern. For others it is not so clear. Part of this book deals with how to make sense of a calling to a particular profession. It addresses a number of questions such as: How do I know what my calling is? Can our calling change? Is our calling always to a profession?

Discerning a calling can be extraordinarily challenging as many of the authors can attest. Many of the chapter authors are doing something quite different from what they initially thought they were called to do. One aspiring market titan is managing an investment firm in Africa. Others discovered their calling during the detours on the way to achieving what they thought their calling was. A Russia expert/aspiring spy is teaching philosophy at a small liberal arts college in suburban Chicago. That is not to discount that they were called, but perhaps their understanding of that call was incomplete. The truth may be that we live life forwards but we only fully discern our calling looking backwards. This may be somewhat reassuring but is not particularly helpful when we are trying to work out which vocational direction to select. However, as the authors such as Howard Louthan attest, in the messiness of discerning our calling, the one constant is God's steady hand.

For other Christians the idea of calling will seem like a distant fantasy unless the scope of calling is expanded beyond our narrow Western ideas. How many Christians are unemployed or doing jobs they did not choose and do not prefer? In the scope of history and in the breadth of the world's human geography only a tiny fraction of the Earth's population has been able to choose a profession or contemplate to which field God was calling them. Today, for example, few children in portions of Indonesia or Central America can realistically contemplate a career in worldwide finance or the arts. They are fortunate if they are able to attend elementary school. Many begin working as soon as they can effectively wield a hoe or carry a load. Others marry and begin domestic work. Their life path is largely set for them by the time and place where they are born and forces outside their control.

Does this mean that God has not placed a calling on their lives? Absolutely not! God's calling on their lives is shaped by their context. For many, and perhaps for all of us, the calling, or callings, may be to minister to parents, neighbors, or the local church. Should we understand lives lived in faithfulness to these callings as less successful? The answer to this question depends upon our definition of success. As Laura Yoder reminds us, "God does not value a university graduate above an illiterate farmer. If the whole earth belongs to

God, the land of a mountaintop community in East Timor is as precious as Manhattan." If the people of rural East Timor and the people of Manhattan are equally precious to God and their circumstances are so different, what does this imply for our understanding of calling and vocation? First, our calling to the local church, to the needy, and our neighbors is usually a much clearer calling than a calling to a specific profession; and for some it may be the only calling we ever hear. This challenges the idea of a singular calling to a career. It would seem that we have what Os Guiness refers to as multiple callings and the temptation is to privilege the calling of career over the seemingly more mundane callings to serve the church, our families and friends (Os Guiness, The Call). Second, what God considers successful probably has less to do with wealth, fame, publications, and recognized disciplinary excellence than we might have thought. After all, there is not always a lot of fame derived from serving your church. Lives lived in relationship with him and in faithfulness to him in different contexts are what he considers successful. And that is our primary call.

2. Faith and Ambition

Yet, for many of us we cannot help feeling a desire, if not a call, to do what is required to reach the top of our professions. Is this from heaven or from hell? Are these aspirations wrong? How hard can we work at it? What are we allowed to sacrifice for it? What if our professional obligations interfere with our ability to raise our families or participate in service to the church? These are hard questions confronted by the authors in various chapters. Many describe the conscious sacrifices made to fulfill another calling on their lives. Matthew Cabeen details the very deliberate decisions he and his wife have taken to raise their family the way they feel called. Laura Yoder describes vividly the choices she made to view interruptions to her research and teaching as callings in their own right. She notes, "How willing am I to view this interrupting situation as potentially more important work than what I had scheduled and planned for the day? On a broader scale, how willing am I to set aside my predetermined professional aspirations to be with people who have experienced tremendous interruption to every aspect of their lives?" One answer to the question of how to reconcile faith and ambition is to ask to what have we been called and for what are we ambitious?

For many Christians that struggle with reconciling their faith and professional ambition, success provides a primary source of satisfaction. Success in our work provides a tangible sense of worth and meaning. It feels great to be recognized. It is comforting to have markers of our accomplishments along the way, a seminal publication, a tenured position, a promotion, or a national award. We like to be deferred to and publicly praised. We are creatures that crave worth and to have been judged worthy. If we are honest with ourselves, our headlong rush for disciplinary excellence or success in our primary vocation can often be a way of proving our worth and demonstrating our value. We want our various audiences—peers, families, churches, the media, history—to tell us we have value. As Nathan Grills explains, citing his interactions with Rhodes scholars, this deep-seated insecurity is an incredible motivator and a heavy yoke.

Grills explains the phenomenon by likening professional success to a drug. It provides us a high for a short period of time but then we need another hit and then another. Once we have accomplished our goal, this feels good for a time and then we are searching again. As an example, Christians in academia pursue tenure with the belief that this will provide a measure of happiness and prestige. It does provide these things to some extent--at least for a while. Yet, many Christians who have achieved tenure spend the years after tenure trying to prove it was a good decision or working to achieve the next professional benchmark. More difficult, some spend the post-tenure years trying to maintain their position in their discipline, to stay on the cutting edge. Once you have achieved respect and notoriety, you do not want to lose or be supplanted by another. Alternatively, the disappointed sometimes use the freedom tenure provides to find contentment in other pursuits. Ultimately, our successes do not provide the lasting sense of worth and validation we crave. We will come up empty.

Christians are confronted with options for dealing with this deep-seated desire for affirmation. One is the headlong pursuit for worth in the opinion of others. Another is to accept that Christ has deemed us valuable and taken away our need to prove anything to anyone. As Paul writes, "I care very little if I am judged by you or by any human court; indeed, I do not even judge myself. My conscience is clear, but that does not make me innocent. It is the Lord who judges me" (1 Cor. 4:3-4; NIV). Fortunately for us, our judge looks at Christ when we are evaluated. This leads Paul to a fundamental conclusion, of central relevance to this book, that he counts all else as loss compared to the greatness of knowing Christ. Knowing Christ is our primary calling and when our 'calling' or ambition interferes with this then it is from hell and not from heaven.

God's intention for us, reflected in how we are created, is that we experience tremendous joy when we accept our value in him and are freed from the burden of seeking our worth from our work. In this light perhaps failure is a severe mercy? Christ loves us too much to allow us to be fooled into thinking that our deepest needs are met. If all that we had was stripped away, we would still have the same value. If, in some sad string of events, our wealth was taken away, all of our accomplishments were revealed as some big mistake, and our treasured relationships with children, family, and friends went south, we would still be valuable and our lives could still be successful. Think about that for a minute. If everything that defines you and makes you feel good about yourself in the presence of other people was stripped away, you would still be valuable and your life could still be successful. What determines your value is God himself, who knows all and loves with a deep and enduring love. In the court of his opinion, you have been deemed innocent, worthy, and loved. There is an enormous freedom in having nothing to lose and nothing to prove. We are free to love well and take risks and experience joy. This is the promise that a number of the chapters reveal for us.

There are two other aspects of reconciling faith and ambition worth mentioning here. For a number of readers, reconciling faith and ambition involves figuring out what to do with personal ambition. The temptation is to be ambitious for personal aggrandizement. For another set, it must be said, the temptation is to use the life of faith to justify mediocrity. We rationalize distraction or poor effort toward our occupation with an appeal to the demands of faith. To use a small example, Christians can spend extra time in Bible study preparation in order to defer doing the secular work required of them. The desire to spend more time in Bible study is laudable except when the purpose is more to avoid doing other things that God has called you to. On a larger scale, Christians might disengage from the responsibilities of work and pursuit of professional excellence because it is difficult and unpleasant. Our pursuit of more work to do for God – even though God did not ask us to do it—can be driven by a desire to rationalize our poor performance at work. When we do not consider what our faith requires of us in our workplace we are more prone to be neglectful of it. If we are clumsy in integrating faith and our work this does not reflect well on Christ and is disobedient. As the apostle Paul teaches in Colossians 3, verses 23-24 "Whatever you do, work at it with all your heart, as working for the Lord, not for men, since you know that you will receive an inheritance from the Lord as a reward. It is the Lord Christ you are serving." In whatever we do, there is no excuse for deliberate laziness.

So, when do we sacrifice activities that lead to professional excellence such as studying, extra time in the studio, and business trips in order to pursue God's call to service in the church and family? And when do we sacrifice opportunities to serve in the church and time with family in order to pursue God's call to our profession? One answer some Christians give to these questions is that there are never sacrifices to be made either way. Perhaps in a rightly ordered life, clear rules can dictate our practice. In our experience this is an unrealistic view. The director of one of our institutes, was both brutal and realistic when he said "I am not advocating that you work every evening and all weekend, but the reality is that you are competing for highly competitive grants with people who are prepared to work those hours." These chapters are filled with examples of authors describing how the demands of profession and family and other Christian service conflict. Life is messy and a properly ordered life includes interruptions and the call to be with people whose lives have been interrupted in ways that are inconvenient for us.

Another answer Christians give to these questions is that God always prefers that Christians sacrifice their 'secular' work for their 'sacred' work in the church. This answer is unsatisfying since it is based upon the false view that God does not call people to a particular profession and our secular work is not part of how a person serves God. Admittedly, local churches atrophy because parishioners rarely understand their calling to work in the local church and we have found few Christian professionals who feel contented with the quality of their parenting. Surely, the global church would be better off if persons spent more time serving the local church and their families? And, for some, God's call may be to yield their professional identity and to sacrifice success at work in order to spend a greater proportion of time serving in church. This is a worthy end, and one strongly advocated in the chapter by Justin Denholm. Yet, God's work also importantly includes work done well for its own sake, for the art that reveals something about the human condition, that provokes the viewer and invites her into a conversation. It includes computer code elegantly written, not because the program is a Christian program but for its own sake. It includes research cleanly and beautifully done, not because it deals with religious topics but because it both pursues truth and is beautiful in its own right. Let us be honest, doing excellent work requires time and thinking, passion and love.

The life of faith, then, places demands upon our work, friendships, churches, and communities. So, how do we reconcile the demands of excellence in work as part of God's overall calling on our lives? In our experience there are few easy rules to guide us. Rather, people will often have a tendency toward one type of error or the other—work at the expense of a life of faith or faith as an excuse for not being faithful in work. The proper allocation of effort across these different activities can only be accomplished by an honest desire to serve God, the immediate guidance of the Holy Spirit, consultation with those whom our decisions affect (in particular our spouse), and the advice of other Christians who know us and love us well. Ultimately, our motives and decisions are often only observable to God and are a personal matter of integrity and faith.

3. God in the Work

Another part of this book presumes that we know to what profession God has called us and progresses on to the question of what difference this makes. It can make a tremendous difference. God's redemptive work in the world involves fixing broken things, often referred to by theologians as the cultural mandate. As participants in his redemptive work, followers of Jesus are Christ's instruments in reaching broken people and renewing the institutions of our world, including cultural institutions such as professions. Our presence should sanctify them and provide an opportunity for rethinking and renewing these institutions in a fundamental way.

Integrating faith and work is more than working hard and with integrity. As suggested above, we would be doing well if these characteristics marked our work as distinctive. Yet, integrating faith and work requires more of us. It often requires asking

God what it means to do our work "Christianly." Can our faith influence our approach to furniture design or dance? What about research or international development? There is significant evidence to suggest that the answer to this question is yes. The chapters provide excellent examples of Christians working out their faith in their professions in creative ways. A professor of Islamic law carefully articulates a pedagogy of listening. A hedge fund manager describes his efforts to figure out what could be distinctive about Christian investing. A literary critic meditates on whether/what could be distinctive about Christian literary criticism.

The integration of faith and our professions shapes not only how we do what we do, but what we do. The definition of calling itself is that God has directed us to something specific (i.e., our profession). Even within professions, our faith can influence what we do. For example, the performance artist might be provoked to create a project about exclusion and embrace. A politician sensitized to God's heart for the widow and the orphan may focus more attention on issues of social justice and care for the marginalized.

In some professions the connection between faith and what we do may be less evident. This is not to suggest, for example, that the Christian literary critic has access to some privileged information or the Christian chemist does a different kind of research. Rather, more simply, the Christian in these professions has invited God into the fundamental choices, the first things of the work. This can take a number of forms such as: •

- Lord, what do you want me to do?
- Why do you want me to do it?

- Lord, please give me wisdom in choosing project A or project B.
- Lord, will you be with me from the choice to start this project through the whole process?

These inclinations of the heart provide a space for God to glorify himself in the worker and the work.

There are two virtues involved in inviting God to be a part of the choices about what to do. First, it provides an opportunity for God to help Christians evaluate and rethink the first things of their professions. For example, it can force us to wrestle with what it means to be a literary critic or how investing and hedge fund management fit into God's purposes for the world. It forces us to ask "What are God's purposes for business or government or culture?" This can be part of God's larger redemptive purposes. When God motivates us to challenge norms and values that do not glorify him, we manifest Christ in our work, and in doing so we are a witness for him in our professions.

Second, inviting God into the choices about what we do also prevents us from believing that the tasks and projects that ultimately become accomplishments are somehow separate from our relationship with God. Many Christians are tempted to identify what they have built or what they have created or what they have written or what they have discovered with themselves. The product of their work or their success is precisely that: their product and their success, not God's. The choice and execution of work is a means of carving out worth and value for ourselves apart from God. If we are honest, we may thank God for these accomplishments but it is hard to do so honestly because *we* did the work. When God is in the process from before it began we can thank God more honestly for his goodness and more easily fit the life of work into our relationship with God. We know of two Ivy League professors who prayed regularly that God would provide them good ideas, the currency of professional success for faculty in research universities. When God answered those prayers and the publications and accolades came, it was more natural to give God the credit because they remembered what it was like before they had those ideas. When ideas did not come or projects did not pan out, they took confidence in knowing that God was aware of their situation and their need. Nothing had happened apart from his notice and involvement.

This is not to suggest this is easy. The chapters, on the contrary, suggest that integrating faith and work is a lifetime endeavor that begins with inclination and is often uncertain and clumsy. It also looks different across contexts and people. Chapter authors describe halting, messy steps in the direction of figuring out what it means to integrate faith into professional careers. For some, a plan for how to integrate faith and work has more or less come together over time. Others are still working out what faith means in their context and they describe their struggles honestly. For yet others, work only gained a visible redemptive coherence over time. God was moving them in a direction but they did not realize it until well afterward. At other times we might misinterpret circumstances as God's leading only to later realize it was clearly not.

Interestingly, there is a commonness and difference that both manifest themselves in the authors' efforts to integrate faith and work. For example, what it means to do work faithfully in the field in Indonesia is different than in a studio in Los

Angeles. This does not mean that the lessons from these experiences do not translate but it does mean that being faithful in these contexts looks different. From working in disaster zones in Indonesia and East Timor, Yoder learns about a ministry of interruptibility, which could inform an approach to work in affluent Los Angeles. Understanding the feeling of being a stranger in between two worlds can resonate in East Timor just as much as Los Angeles. The presence of the Holy Spirit is recognizable and familiar across contexts but His manifestation is different in field research and painting.

Although we all have the same Spirit we work in different professions and contexts and this shapes what it looks like to integrate faith into our work lives. Additionally, we are each uniquely created with different gifts, and who we are influences how we as Christians respond to different contexts. People actively seeking God in their professional lives will embody models of integration that are quite different from one another simply because the people themselves are different. For example, there are several professors that contributed chapters to this book. One professor has put into practice a beautiful and demanding pedagogy that reflects the love of Christ for the other. Another describes ways that he invites God into the research process. A third discusses the Christian as dissident and the involvement of Christian faculty in the activities of Christian groups on campus. Each is inclined toward God but they reflect God's redemptive purposes in different ways.

4. Faithful is Successful

Another common experience connects the chapter authors. The authors work in fields where there are few Christians. This influences how they are perceived at work and indeed within the church. It can be quite alienating because people in the church will misunderstand and undervalue work to which other Christians have been called. For example, Sarah Awad describes how difficult it is to be an artist and a Christian. Artists and critics often stereotype and misunderstand Christians and Christians frequently shun or misunderstand modern art. Other Christians called to fields where there are few Christians are assumed to have done nothing for God if they have not shared the gospel at work, as if their participation in their work faithfully and well is not a means of participating in God's care and plan for the world.

Other authors describe the tremendous pressure for professional success that comes from different quarters, including family and the church. Justin Denholm relates, "On our way out of the service that morning, the pastor said something to my parents that has haunted me ever since: he told them that he was sure that God had prepared me to do 'great things' with my life. Great things? Me? What counts as 'great'?" The pressure is multiplied by churches falling into the trap outlined above in which they esteem earthly success at work because that will most effectively reveal God to the world. A number of authors in this book describe the pressure to do something "great" in the world precisely because of their unique talents and abilities, as if the success or failure of God's kingdom depended upon their choices and ultimate success.

The contributors to this edited volume have impressive credentials but few, if any, would describe their career path as going from glory to glory. Indeed, a number of the authors explain how they have learned that "success," in God's economy, may, at times, mean learning to fail faithfully. For example, a faithful man or woman might refuse a promotion or job change, and so fail in the world's eyes, in order to continue serving at church or in the family. For the Christian being faithful, in success and in failure, is what is successful.

Most of the authors will tell you that their life has been at points lonely and confusing. Most will also tell you that their path has been littered with some combination of professional and moral failure. The authors have had the common experience of working incredibly hard for something and failing. It might be a failed business. It might be missing out on the prestigious research career. For some, the toil and challenge took a toll on their marriage, friendships and faith. It is not uncommon for the drive for success to lead to moral compromise. Deeper conversations with these authors would reveal cases where they hid their faith because they were embarrassed, failed in their parenting in non-trivial ways, or did not meet the highest ethical standards in their work. They would volunteer their many failings, both professional and moral.

Fortunately, the gospel message has very little to do with our own perfection or professional success. Rather, it is for everyone, particularly the sinners and failures. Woven into these chapters is a deep sense of gratitude and joy in the midst of everything. This stems from the fact that the authors have come to know, often through their failures, that their ultimate value and significance comes from Christ, rather than their resume. The authors do not write because they have everything figured out. They write because their experience trying to follow Christ might help someone else.

Author Biographies

Sarah Awad lives and works in Los Angeles. She received an MFA in painting from University of California, Los Angeles. Her work has been exhibited in solo and group exhibitions at Diane Rosenstein and LA Louver in Los Angeles, James Harris Gallery in Seattle and the Torrance Art Museum, among others. Awad has been featured in the Los Angeles Times and was the 2011 recipient of a Joan Mitchell Foundation Grant. In addition to exhibiting, she teaches painting and drawing at Art Center College of Design.

Matthew Cabeen is a postdoctoral fellow of the Jane Coffin Childs Foundation studying in the Department of Molecular and Cellular Biology at Harvard University. He studies bacterial community behavior in Bacillus subtilis and Pseudomonas aeruginosa in the laboratory of Prof. Richard Losick. He conducted his doctoral studies with Professor Christine Jacobs-Wagner in the Department of Molecular, Cellular & Developmental Biology at Yale University. He is the author of several articles about bacterial cell shape and the bacterial cytoskeleton. Matt lives with his wife, Rose, and their three young sons, Tommy, Benjamin, and Henry, in Boston, Massachusetts. The Cabeens attend church at their local Roman Catholic parish, St. Ann.

Justin Denholm lives in Brunswick, Australia with his wife, three children and two chickens, where he has many challenging conversations about faith and life. Since 2008, he has coordinated the Centre for Applied Christian Ethics at Ridley Melbourne Mission and Ministry College, which concentrates on providing resources and support for Christians to engage with ethical issues in all aspects of life. Justin also works as an infectious diseases physician and epidemiologist at the Royal Melbourne Hospital, Australia, where his clinical and research interests are focused on tuberculosis and other communicable diseases. He holds degrees in medicine, ethics, public health and epidemiology, and is actively involved in teaching programs for these subjects at the University of Melbourne. He has written or edited several books, including most recently a Christian guide to having better ethical discussions: *Talking About Ethics: Negotiating the Maze* (Acorn Press, 2011).

Dr. Nathan Grills is a Public Health Physician at the Nossal Institute of Global Health (University of Melbourne) and is working in disability and chronic disease prevention in India and undertaking social network analysis exploring cooperation between health NGOs. He is supported by an Australian government postdoctoral fellowship and he has an honorary academic appointment with the Public Health Foundation of India (Indian public sector) and faculty role with the Emmanuel Health Association community health section. Nathan completed an MSc Global Health Sciences and then PhD in Public Health at Oxford University where he explored the role of faith in the response of Faith-based groups to HIV. During this time he worked with the Centers for Disease Control (India) and the World Health Organization

Headquarters (WHO) exploring civil society partnerships. Dr. Grills is also the International Coordinator of the Community Health Global Network which, amongst other things, has assisted community health NGOs to engage with the WHO.

Bruce Huber is an Associate Professor of Law at the Notre Dame Law School in South Bend, Indiana, where he and his wife, Sarah, are raising their four children. He earned a B.A. in Political Science at Stanford University and a J.D. and Ph.D. in Political Science at the University of California at Berkeley. Before his graduate work, he served for four years as the minister to college students at the Menlo Park Presbyterian Church, an experience which continues to shape his ideas about faith and vocation. Before joining the faculty at Notre Dame in 2011, he taught for two years in the Department of Government at Dartmouth College. His research explores environmental, property, natural resources, and energy law, and he attends the South Bend Christian Reformed Church.

Dano Jukanovich is a co-founder and partner with Karisimbi Business Partners in Kigali, Rwanda, a socially motivated management consulting and private equity firm focused on small and mid-size enterprise development. With more than eighteen years of experience, Dano has held responsibility for business development and finance for start-ups and established companies including AT&T Wireless before accepting the role of CEO for a mid-sized U.S. construction company. His background includes five years of service as a U.S. Army Airborne Ranger and Senior Intelligence Officer prior to application of his leadership to a variety of companies. Dano received his Bachelor of Science degree in Economics from the United States Military Academy at West Point in 1993. As part of his military service, Dano lived in Seoul, Korea and learned Mandarin Chinese while studying in Beijing, China. He also earned his MBA degree with a specialty in Finance at Wharton. That same year, Dano earned a Master of Arts in International Economics & China Studies at the Johns Hopkins Nitze School of Advanced International Studies. Dano also continues in the West Point "soldier-athlete" tradition, having recently completed the 2012 Ironman in South Africa.

David E. Lewis is the William R. Kenan, Jr. professor of political science at Vanderbilt University. His research interests include the presidency, executive branch politics and public administration. He is the author of two books, *Presidents and the Politics of Agency Design* (Stanford University Press, 2003) and *The Politics of Presidential Appointments: Political Control and Bureaucratic Performance* (Princeton University Press, 2008), and numerous articles on American politics, public administration and management. Before joining Vanderbilt's Department of Political Science in fall 2008, he was assistant professor of politics and public affairs at Princeton University, where he was affiliated with the Center for the Study of Democratic Politics, from 2002-08. He began his academic career at the College of William and Mary, where he was an assistant professor in the Department of Government from 2000-02. David and his family attend the Village Chapel in historic Hillsboro Village in Nashville, Tennessee.

Howard Louthan is professor of history at the University of Florida where he teaches with his wife, Andrea Sterk, who is also a member of the history faculty. He specializes in the cultural and intellectual history of Renaissance and Reformation Europe with a particular focus on religion. His most recent books include *Converting Bohemia: Force and Persuasion in the Catholic Reformation* (Cambridge, 2009) and an edited collection of essays *Sacred History: Uses of the Christian Past in the Renaissance World* (Oxford, 2012). Howard and Andrea have a family of three children. In fall 2015 both Howard and Andrea will be assuming new positions at the University of Minnesota.

Bryan McGraw is associate professor politics at Wheaton College. Bryan has always had an interest in the normative and philosophical aspects of politics and discovered political theory only in graduate school. He is particularly interested in the ways modern states seek to establish and enforce their own normative visions and how religion plays into that process. He has taught previously at the University of Georgia, Notre Dame and Pepperdine University. His first book, *Faith in Politics: Religion and Liberal Democracy*, was published by Cambridge University Press, and he is beginning a project on pluralism, law and religion, and political theology. He earned an AM in political science from Brown University, an MA in Russian area studies from Georgetown, and his PhD in political science from Harvard University. Bryan and his wife, Martha, a practicing neurologist, live in Wheaton with their three children. They enjoy gardening, all manners of outdoor activities, and perfecting the art of pulled-pork BBQ sandwiches.

Caleb D. Spencer teaches literary theory, American literature, and aesthetics in the Department of English at Azusa Pacific University. He holds a PhD in English (2011) from the University of Illinois at Chicago where, in addition to his work in literature and literary theory, he focused his research on the intersections between aesthetics, philosophy of language and theology in late modernity. He has twice been a visiting professor of English at Wheaton College where he graduated with a BA in English in 1999. He is currently at work on a monograph entitled Protestant Postmodernism: theory and theology, affect and art on the peculiar ways that late-Modern British and American culture mirrors central features of Protestant Liberalism. The book has chapters on Tillich and postmodernism aesthetics, contemporary conversion and deconversion narratives, films and novels like Fight Club and Twilight, apocalyptic narratives including The Road and Left Behind, the resurgence of theology in contemporary Continental philosophy in the work of Badiou and Zizek, and a critique of the notion that postmodernism is a continuation of the Comteian secularization hypothesis offered by historians of late-Modernity like Fredric Jameson. He is also working on a trade book proposal on professionals who are simultaneously stay-at-home fathers. His scholarly work has been published in the Journal of Religion and Popular Culture, Christianity and Literature, and in various visual art catalogues. Prior to focusing on American literature and theology, he worked on British Romanticism and Milton, including an MA thesis on *Wordsworth's Prelude and the Theology of Romanticism.* In addition to his current academic work, Caleb works as a professional photographer, doing portraits, occasional commercial work and art b&w, and has worked as a clerk in a law firm. He is now bi-vocational as he is a stay-at-home dad to his three children Sophia (9), Auden (5) and Hadley (20 months) while Brooke, his wife of thirteen years, works as a health care executive. He is also involved in avocational ministry as a ruling elder at his Presbyterian church, helping with the arts ministries and as a college and high school ministry leader. Caleb is an avid cyclist, racing on the both road and in cyclocross events.

Soo Chuen Tan is managing member of Discerene Value Advisors LLC, a private investment firm which invests globally pursuing a concentrated, long term, value investment philosophy for several leading university endowments, foundations, and families. Before founding Discerene, Mr. Tan was at Deccan Value Advisors, the Baupost Group, Halcyon Asset Management, and McKinsey & Company. He has an MBA from Harvard Business School where he was a Baker Scholar, and a BA (double first class honors) in Jurisprudence from Oxford University, where he won the Oxford University/ Martin Wronker Prize. Originally from Malaysia, Mr. Tan now lives in Stamford, Connecticut.

David Vishanoff is an associate professor in the Religious Studies program at the University of Oklahoma, where he strives to put his theory of sacrificial listening into practice in both teaching and scholarship. He earned a B.A. in mathematics and philosophy at Gordon College, an M.A. in religious studies at the University of Colorado, and a Ph.D. in Islamic thought at Emory University. His research is principally concerned with how religious people interpret and conceptualize sacred texts—both their own, and those of other religious traditions. He has published several articles on Islamic versions of the Psalms of David, and a monograph titled *The Formation of Islamic Hermeneutics: How Sunni Legal Theorists Imagined a Revealed Law*. He is beginning to study contemporary Islamic hermeneutical thought, and writing introductory textbooks on Islamic legal theory and Islamic theology. He lives in Norman, Oklahoma with his wife, their two teenagers, his parents, and his mother-in-law, in a large home that often welcomes students and friends from church.

Laura Meitzner Yoder enjoys learning and teaching about how people make claims to the natural world and how human societies negotiate using and sharing what we claim. She draws inspiration and hope from over a decade spent with smallholder farmers and forest dwellers in Latin America and Southeast Asia, as they work out their access to land and forests. Most of her overseas positions have bridged the worlds of rural villages and a local university, teaching plant sciences, field research methods, social forestry, political ecology, and environmental anthropology. She directs the program in Human Needs and Global Resources (HNGR) and is associate professor of environmental science at Wheaton College, Illinois, USA, and continues to spend time each year in Asia with her husband and son. Her publications address topics including the interaction of state and customary authorities in resource regulation, agricultural improvements in marginal production areas, international development initiatives, environmental justice, and institutions that govern the commons.

CPSIA information can be obtained
at www.ICGtesting.com
Printed in the USA
BVHW071500040522
636050BV00001B/22